# ESSENTIAL DOMINICAN REPUBLIC

**Original text by Lee Karen Stowe**
Updated by Lindsay Bennett

© AA Media Limited 2008
First published 2008. Reprinted 2010

ISBN 978-0-7495-6673-9

Published by AA Publishing, a trading name of AA Media Limited, whose registered office is Fanum House, Basing View, Basingstoke, Hampshire RG21 4EA. Registered number 06112600.

Colour separation: MRM Graphics Ltd
Printed and bound in Italy by Printer Trento S.r.l.

A04192
Maps in this title produced from mapping © MAIRDUMONT/Falk Verlag 2010
Additional data from Mountain High Maps® Copyright © 1993 Digital Wisdom, Inc

# About this book

This book is divided into six sections.

**The essence of the Dominican Republic** pages 6–19
Introduction; Features; Food and drink; Short break including the 10 Essentials

**Planning** pages 20–33
Before you go; Getting there; Getting around; Being there

**Best places to see** pages 34–55
The unmissable highlights of any visit to the Dominican Republic

**Best things to do** pages 56–79
Great cafés; Stunning views; Places to take the children and more

**Exploring** pages 80–154
The best places to visit in the Dominican Republic, organized by area

❖ to ❖❖❖❖ denotes AAA rating

**Maps**
All map references are to the maps on the covers. For example, Puerto Plata has the reference ➕ 6B – indicating the grid square in which it is to be found

**Admission prices**
Inexpensive (under RD$3)
Moderate (RD$4–RD$8)
Expensive (over RD$8)

**Hotel prices**
Price are per room per night: $ budget (under RD$2,750); $$ moderate (RD$2,750–5,500); $$$ expensive to luxury (over RD$5,500)

**Restaurant prices**
Price for a three-course meal per person without drinks: $ budget (under RD$500); $$ moderate (RD$500–900); $$$ expensive (over RD$900)

# Contents

BEST THINGS TO DO

EXPLORING…

56 – 79   80 – 185

# The essence of...

The Dominican Republic ticks all the boxes in a shortlist of natural requirements for the perfect holiday. Visually stunning, it offers myriad dreamy golden beaches lapped by shimmering waters, capped by azure skies, and backed by gently swaying luscious palms. The sun sizzles by day, and the heat lingers into balmy nights.

features

The Dominican Republic shares Hispaniola, the largest island in the Caribbean, with Haiti and its sheer size gives it a diversity rarely found in the rest of the region, with verdant jungles, dry deserts and true mountain ranges.

Over the last twenty years, tourism has really taken off, and the international hotel groups have flocked to create magnificent resorts. Take your pick – from spas to adrenalin sports. It's one of the world's best locations for windsurfing and kite-surfing, or play a round of golf on some of the most challenging greens around. It's a playground for the animal world too, with much of the world's population of hump-back whales congregating in the offshore waters between January and March.

When Christopher Columbus landed here in 1492 he wasn't looking for a little R&R but the riches of the Orient. He founded the city of Santo Domingo, now the country's capital, with a central core little changed over the intervening centuries. Walk the alleyways and boulevards here to feel the essence of the "New World."

Dominicans have a zest for life that's almost palpable, felt in the erotic beat of the merengue music that fills the streets and seen in the vibrant naïve art on sale in galleries across the country. Enjoy the undoubted pleasures of your hotel but

leave plenty for time to get under the skin of this fascinating destination.

## GEOGRAPHY

● The Dominican Republic occupies part of the larger island of Hispaniola, which it shares with Haiti.
● The area of the Dominican Republic is 18,814 sq miles/48,730 sq km (approx 66 percent of the area of Hispaniola). Its land boundary with Haiti is 179 miles (275km) long and its coastline is 800 miles (1,288km) long.
● The interior is blanketed with rugged mountains and fertile valleys.
● Highest point Pico Duarte at 10,417 ft (3,175m).

## POPULATION

● The country's population is estimated at 8.9 million.
● The earliest inhabitants were Indians from the Amazon basin.
● The Taino Indians who arrived AD 700 were resident at the time of the arrival of the Europeans.
● The current ethnic mix is classed as black 11 percent, white 16 percent and mixed 73 percent.

## ECONOMIC FACTORS

● Service industries (including tourism) contribute 57 percent to national GDP.
● Main industries include tourism, mining, sugar processing and tobacco.
● Estimated households (2003) living below the poverty line 20 percent.

## TOURISM

● Tourist numbers in 2005 reached almost 4 million.
● Between January and April 2006 1,310,015 people arrived at Dominican Republic airports, a 12 percent growth on 2005.

## food & drink

Sticking to the all-inclusive buffet just because you've paid for it doesn't mean you can't be adventurous one day and eat out. Dominican food is nothing if not varied, handed down from the Spanish colonizers, indigenous Indians and African slaves.

In the capital, Santo Domingo, Japanese sushi bars rub shoulders with French cuisine and clay-oven baked pizzas. What you get is a basic melting pot with cassava, sweet potato, bean, fish, spices, carrots, artichokes and bananas to name a few, jazzed up with fashionable trends.

### MEALS

Breakfast can be muffins, waffles and *Café Santo Domingo* at the patisseries of Cabarete, or eggs and *mangú* (mashed plantains and onions) served

at a beach bar. The main meal is lunch, maybe *la bandera* – a mix of rice with red beans and meats – followed by a blissful siesta. The national dish is *sancocho*, a stew made with pork, beef, chicken or goat and vegetables, with a round of cassava bread. (In the Dominican Alps you can see cassava bread being made by hand in the Taino way.)

## SEAFOOD

Dominican seafood is absolutely superb, ranging from grilled shrimp and lobster to sea bass and kingfish. *Pescado con coco* is fish cooked in a delicious coconut and cream sauce. The meat of the conch shell *(lambi)*, usually marinated and served with salad, is thought to be an aphrodisiac.

## DRINKS

An ideal cure for a hangover is *guarapo*, thick sugarcane juice. To need it in the first place, try "151 Rum" – 75 proof! *Ron* (rum) is, of course, the national drink. It comes in light, golden, or dark and aged varieties. The most popular brands are Brugal, Bermudez and Barceló. Presidente beer is advertized everywhere and is best drunk ice cold from the bottle. Cocktails are plentiful. Cuba Libre is rum and coke, a coco-loco is coconut milk and rum actually served in the coconut, and a Banana Mama is a non-alcoholic cocktail – banana with fresh fruits and grenadine. Other non-alcoholic drinks popular

with Dominicans are orange juice (which they sweeten heavily with sugar) and fruit punch. Although known brands of soft drinks are sold, an instant refresher is a *tierno*, a soft coconut bought by the roadside. After drinking its juice through a straw, find a spoon and devour the succulent flesh.

short break

If you only have a short time to visit the Dominican Republic and would like to take home some unforgettable memories, the following suggestions will give you a wide range of sights and experiences that won't take long, won't cost very much and will make your visit very special.

● **Walk the cobbled streets** of the historic **Zona Colonial** in the capital, Santo Domingo, where the Spanish conquistadors established their mighty seat in the New World (➤ 54).

• **Spot American crocodiles and pink flamingos** at Lago Enriquillo (Lake Enriquillo) and don't forget a camera (➤ 44).

• **Laze on the white sands** of the Atlantic coast, doing nothing more than ordering rum punches.

• **Learn to dance** *merengue* **like a Dominican,** then get totally carried away on the dance floor.

● **Go whale-watching** in the Bahía de Samaná (Samana Bay) (➤ 38) and watch humpback whales breach spectacularly from the ocean (➤ 39).

● **Take a speedboat** through crystal waters to Isla Saona (Saona Island) (➤ 42) in the Parque Nacional de la Este (National Park of the East) (➤ 129) to swim, then eat grilled lobster beneath the shade of a palm.

● **Learn to windsurf** with the experts on world-famous Cabarete beach (➤ 106).

● **Breathe in the invigorating alpine air** in the foothills of Pico Duarte, the Caribbean's tallest mountain (➤ 41).

● **Have your hair braided** and adorned with beads. Yes, men too. And don't forget to barter.

● **Watch cigars being made** at tobacco museums in the Cibao Valley, then buy one to smoke after dinner.

# Planning

# Before you go

## WHEN TO GO

| JAN | FEB | MAR | APR | MAY | JUN | JUL | AUG | SEP | OCT | NOV | DEC |
|-----|-----|-----|-----|-----|-----|-----|-----|-----|-----|-----|-----|
| 25°C | 25°C | 25°C | 25°C | 25°C | 28°C | 28°C | 28°C | 28°C | 28°C | 25°C | 26°C |
| 77°F | 77°F | 77°F | 77°F | 77°F | 82°F | 82°F | 82°F | 82°F | 82°F | 77°F | 79°F |

🔴 Low season   ⚪ High season

The Dominican Republic has fairly stable temperatures throughout the year, usually around 80°F (high-20s°C). The main tourist season is Nov-Apr when temperatures and humidity are generally at their lowest. The rainy season runs from May to October, when temperatures rise slightly but humidity is high due to the short, sharp downpours.

The rainy season is overlapped by the hurricane season, which officially lasts from June to November, though most storms occur between August and October, and not every season brings a hurricane. Hurricanes are violent but short-lived storms that can cause tremendous damage, however, in the Caribbean there is a well practised warning system.

The temperatures given above are the average daily maximum for each month.

## WHAT YOU NEED

| | | UK | Germany | USA | Netherlands | Spain |
|---|---|---|---|---|---|---|
| ● | Required | | | | | |
| ○ | Suggested | Some countries require a passport to remain valid for a minimum period (usually at least six months) beyond the date of entry – check before you travel. | | | | |
| ▲ | Not required | | | | | |
| Passport (for stay of less than 90 days) | | ● | ● | ● | ● | ● |
| Tourist card (US$10 payable on arrival, must be paid in US$) | | ● | ● | ● | ● | ● |
| Onward or Return Ticket | | ▲ | ▲ | ▲ | ▲ | ▲ |
| Health Inoculations (polio, tetanus, typhoid, hepatitis A) | | ○ | ○ | ○ | ○ | ○ |
| Health Documentation (▶ 23, Health Insurance) | | ▲ | ▲ | ▲ | ▲ | ▲ |
| Travel Insurance | | ○ | ○ | ○ | ○ | ○ |
| Driving Licence (national with Spanish translation or international) | | ● | ● | ● | ● | ● |
| Car Insurance Certificate | | ○ | ○ | ○ | ○ | ○ |
| Car Registration Document | | n/a | n/a | n/a | n/a | n/a |

## WEBSITES
The official portal for the Dominican Republic is:
www.dominicanrepublic.com

## TOURIST OFFICES AT HOME

### In the UK
18–21 Hand Court
High Holborn, London
WC1V 6JE
☎ 020 7242 7778

### In the USA
E 57th Street, Suite 803
136 New York, NY 10022
☎ 212 588 1012/13/14
Toll Free 1 888 374 6361

## HEALTH INSURANCE
A doctor is on call at major hotels. These are stocked with medicine for the most common ailments. Ambulances are available, as is air ambulance evacuation ☎ 911. Emergency dental treatment can be provided.

## TIME DIFFERENCES

| GMT | Dominican | Germany | USA (NY) | Netherlands | Spain |
| --- | --- | --- | --- | --- | --- |
| 12 noon | Republic 8AM | 1PM | 7AM | 1PM | 1PM |

The Dominican Republic is four hours behind Greenwich Mean Time and does not operate a system of daylight savings time.

## NATIONAL HOLIDAYS
1 Jan *New Year's Day*
21 Jan *Day of Our Lady of Altagracia*
Jan 26 (celebrated closest Mon or Fri) *Duarte Day*
Jan 27 *Independence Day*
Mar/Apr *Good Friday and Easter Monday*

16 Aug (celebrated closest Monday or Fri) *Restoration Day*
24 Sep *Day of Our Lady of Mercedes*
6 Nov (celebrated closest Monday or Fri) *Constitution Day*

15 Dec *Christmas Day*

Most banks, businesses, museums and shops are closed on these days.

## WHAT'S ON WHEN

**January** Jan. 21: *Virgin of La Altagracia day.* This is a major pilgrimage to Basílica de Nuestra Señora de la Altagracia in Higüey, where the Virgin Mary supposedly appeared in 1691 (and many times since).
Jan.26 (or closest Monday or Friday): *Juan Pablo Duarte's birthday.* Carnival fever grips the country, leading up to National Independence Day celebrations (February).

**February** Feb. 27 (or last Sunday of the month): *National Independence Day* is a massive holiday celebrating the day in 1844 when Juan Pablo Duarte, Francisco del Rosario Sánchez and Ramón Matías Mella overthrew the occupying Haitians. Raising the three-colored flag of the nation (navy, red and white) they declared independence at Puerto del Conde (Gate of Entrance) in El Conde street, in the historic Zona Colonial.

Celebrations usually begin on Jan. 26, birthday of Duarte, and continue to the big day. If you're there, head down to Avenue George Washington in Santo Domingo. Locals form a corridor between the seafront and the city and representatives of the country's national fighting force parade through, from commandos to fighter pilots. Police squads and troops, together with tanks, guns and military vehicles, pass in front of the president, while aircraft drop parachutists in a dramatic finale.

The northwest town of Monte Cristi hosts the *El Morro Carnival* featuring a person acting as an evil, angry bull who has a mock battle with the good civilians. People dance in the street, eat, drink, and later consume quantities of sugarcane juice to relieve their hangovers.

**June** In Puerto Plata, at the foot of Fuerte de San Felipe, a week-long Cultural Festival is held featuring blues, jazz, salsa and *merengue*. Dancers and musicians from around the country drop by to perform for the crowds. The Cabarete Race Week (an international windsurfing competition) is held each June.

**July** Third week: A notable *merengue* festival along the *malécon* (seafront promenade) in Santo Domingo. Singers and dancers compete for prizes for the best live performances. The festival is so popular it has now extended to Boca Chica.

**August** Aug. 16 (or closest Monday or Friday): *Restoration Day*, marking the country's declaration of war with Spain in 1863. Another energetic carnival with elaborate floats and *merengue* dancing.

**October** Puerto Plata's contribution to *merengue* takes off with a festival that smothers the *malécon* with stalls and festivities. Jazz festival around Sosúa and Cabarete.

**December** Early Dec.–Jan. 6: Christmas parties most weekends. Tree branches are painted green and white and decorated with ornaments.

# Getting there

## BY AIR

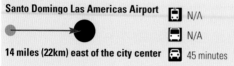

| Santo Domingo Las Americas Airport | | N/A |
| --- | --- | --- |
| | | N/A |
| 14 miles (22km) east of the city center | | 45 minutes |

The Dominican Republic is a large country by Caribbean standards and is served by eight international airports. Major airlines providing scheduled services include American Airlines (www.aa.com), Iberia (www.iberia.com), Delta (www.delta.com), Continental (www.continental.com), Lufthansa (www.lufthansa.com), and Virgin Airlines (www.virgin.com). Most flights from the UK involve at least one transfer in mainland Europe or the USA. To compare current deals try one of the travel websites or your professional travel agent.

Direct flights are provided by the tour operators from the UK who offer flight-only options usually at better prices than the scheduled airlines but these may be limited to one or two week duration. Companies to contact are Thomas Cook (www.thomascook.co.uk), First Choice (www.firstchoice.co.uk) or Airtours (www.airtours.co.uk). You may find that a one or two-week package, including flights and hotels, may offer considerable cost saving when compared to booking the two elements individually. In the UK, contact the above companies; in the US consult a professional travel agent.

Most arriving passengers (including UK, European, and North American citizens) must pay US$10 for a tourist card which allows entry for up to two weeks. This card can be extended for up to three months. You can apply for a tourist card before arrival but this process can take up to three weeks so most visitors buy on arrival. All passengers must pay a US$20 departure tax.

At the time of writing the Dominican Republic had just annouced plans to fund a national airline. Plans have yet to be finalized.

### BY SEA

One commercial ferry company offers services between the Dominican Republic and Mayagüez in Puerto Rico. Ferries del Caribe (tel: 688 4400, www.ferriesdelcaribe.com) have three services per week arriving at Santo Domingo and the crossing takes 12 hours. The only other way to arrival by sea is by cruise liner, on a pre-booked itinerary. Ships normally dock at Casa de Campo, or Samana to take advantage of the whale watching, however, stays are usually limited to just a few hours.

# Getting around

## PUBLIC TRANSPORT

**Internal flights** Air Santo Domingo is a local airline that operates regular scheduled flights between the principal tourist regions of the country: Las Américas Dr. JFPG (Santo Domingo); La Isabela Dr Joaquin Balaguer (Santo Domingo); Gregorio Luperón (Puerto Plata); Arroyo Barril (Samaná); Cibao (Santiago); María Montez (Barahona); Punta Aguila (Romana); Punta Cana (Higüey), El Catey. Reservations ☎ 683 8006.

**Buses** Two bus companies, Metro Services ☎ 566 7126 and Caribe Tours ☎ 221 4422; www.caribetours.com provide excellent transportation between Santo Domingo and major cities. Tickets are exceptionally inexpensive and buses are modern and comfortable with air-conditioning, drinks and sweets. Passengers are advised to reserve seats in advance.

**Gua-guas** A type of mini bus, the *gua-gua* trundles between the country's smaller towns, resorts, and historic sites and is usually weighed down with both locals and tourists. Either board them in the central squares of towns and villages or hail them by the roadside. The low fare is usually paid at your drop-off stop.

**Caro publicos** A cross between a *gua-gua* and a taxi, *carros públicos* are cars that operate on a set route and will pick up and drop off anywhere en-route.

## FARES AND TICKETS

By bus from Santo Domingo from Sosua costs RD$250, and from Santo Domingo to Puerto Plata costs RD$215. Tickets can be bought from the company terminals (Caribe Tours at Avenida 27 de Febrero, Metro at Calle Francisco Ramirez) and though you don't need to book in advance, it is wise to arrive and pay at least 30 minutes before departure.

*Gua-guas* charge approximately RD$10 for a short journey (up to 5 miles/8km). Try to find out how much the fare should be if you intend to travel further. There are no tickets and payment is taken as your journey finishes. Try to have small denominations or exact fare if possible.

## TAXIS

Private taxis are available 24 hours a day in Santo Domingo, Santiago and Puerto Plata and the larger hotels. Public taxis *(carros públicos)* are similar to *gua-guas* and have to be signaled to stop. Spotlessly clean cream taxis are seen hanging around tourist sites. Although more expensive they offer a comfortable sightseeing alternative. Many drivers speak English. There are no meters, just set rates, so you must negotiate the fare in advance.

## DRIVING

- Drive on the right in the Dominican Republic.
- Seat belts are legally required, although you'll see the locals without them. Unsurfaced roads and manic drivers make the Dominican Republic a hazardous place to drive. Exercise caution at all times and always wear a seat belt, regardless of what anyone else is doing. Beware of corrupt domestic traffic police that have a habit of stopping you for a dubious offence, demanding an on-the-spot fine. Driving at night should be avoided.
- Never drive under the influence of alcohol. You may find that your insurance coverage is not valid for accidents due to alcohol.
- Gas stations *(bombas)* are open until 6pm or in larger towns 10pm. The main resorts and towns have 24-hour gas stations but might be closed on Sundays. Fuel prices fluctuate widely. Fuel *(gasolina)* is available in diesel, unleaded, regular and regular supreme.
- Speed limits are as follows:
  on motorways: 50–62mph (80–100kph)
  on main roads: 37mph (60kph)
  on minor roads: 25mph (40kph)

## CAR RENTAL

As a last resort, instead of using safer buses and organized tours, you can rent a car (age 25–65). Major car rental companies have airport and city locations. A valid driver's licence and major credit car is required. When renting car, check and double check the insurance regulations. Accidents can be a very costly business and if you're a foreigner you may have problems proving your case.

To leave Santo Domingo drivers have to pay 15 pesos at exit points.

# Being there

## TOURIST OFFICES

There are small tourist offices in many major towns, but not in all tourist areas.

The main tourist office in Santo Domingo is at:
Calle Isabel la Catolica 103
Zona Colonial
☎ 686 3858

**In the UK**
18/22 Hand Court
High Holborn
London
WC1V 6JE
☎ 020 7242 7778

**In the USA**
E 57th Street, Suite 803
136 New York
NY 10022
Toll Free 1 888 374 6361
☎ 212 588 1012/13/14

## MONEY

The Dominican monetary unit is the peso (RD$ or DOP) divided into 100 centavos. Foreign currency can be changed at exchange booths of the Banco de Reservas at airports, major hotels or commercial banks. Banking hours are 8:30am to 6pm, Monday to Friday. Airport booths remain open to service all incoming flights, up to 24 hours if necessary. Traveler's checks and major credit cards are widely accepted. Cash advances are available at some commercial banks.

## TIPS/GRATUITIES

| Yes ✓     No ✗ | | |
|---|---|---|
| Restaurants (if service not included) | ✓ | 10% |
| Cafés/bars (if service not included) | ✓ | 10% |
| Taxis | ✓ | RD$30–50 |
| Tour guides | ✓ | RD$50–100 |
| Porters/ Chambermaids | ✓ | change |
| Toilet attendants | ✓ | change |

## POSTAL AND INTERNET SERVICES

Though international mail is inexpensive, the postal service is slow and unreliable. For parcels or documents, choose a reliable courier.

There are internet cafés or small communications bureaus with internet access in all the tourist resorts and most of the major towns. Prices are inexpensive, around RD$35-50 per hour.

## TELEPHONES

You can make phone calls from any Verizon or Tricom centers (pay after the call). Pay as you go phone cards for differing denominations are widely available. Call 611 to access English-speaking services. Direct dial to the Dominican Republic by dialling 1 809.

**International dialling codes**
From Dominican Republic to
UK: 0 11 44
Germany: 0 11 49
USA and Canada: 0 1
Netherlands: 0 11 31
Spain: 0 11 34

**Emergency telephone numbers**
Police: 911
Fire: 911
Ambulance: 911
Tourist police: 686 8639
(toll free 1 200 3500)

## EMBASSIES AND CONSULATES

UK ☎ 472 7111
Germany ☎ 542 8949

USA ☎ 221 2171
Spain ☎ 535 6500

## HEALTH ADVICE

**Sun advice** The Caribbean sun is extremely strong and you must protect your skin. Choose a good-quality, high-factor sunscreen and reapply frequently, especially after swimming and watersports. Avoid the midday sun. Wear good sunglasses and, if possible, a wide-brimmed hat. Limit yourself when first going to the beach. If you do suffer sunburn, stay out of the sun until you recover. If symptoms of headache, nausea or dizziness occur, call a doctor.

**Drugs** Many pharmacies in Santo Domingo are open 24 hours a day. Other pharmacies are located in most cities, towns and villages. Many drugs, including antibiotics, are available without prescription.

**Safe water** Do not drink tap water. Buy bottled water for drinking and brushing teeth and make sure the seal is not broken. If you are unsure about ice in your drinks, go without. Never buy ice or cups of drinking water from a street vendor.

## PERSONAL SAFETY

Store travel documents and valuables in your room or hotel safe. Avoid isolated streets and unfamiliar neighborhoods, especially at night. Avoid driving at night. Beware of black market currency, drugs and prostitution in the major tourist centers. Police: ☎ 911

## ELECTRICITY

Power supply: 110 volts/60 cycles, the same as in the US. Europeans will need an adaptor. Power cuts are not uncommon.

## OPENING HOURS

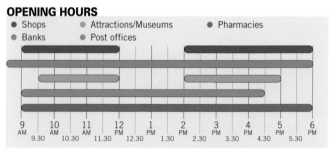

Some stores usually close Saturday at 2pm. Major stores are also open on Sundays until 2pm, some until 10pm. Consulates and embassies are open 8–2. Churches hold weekly services (Santo Domingo's synagogue Friday evenings). There are 24-hour pharmacies in Santo Domingo and some other major cities.

## LANGUAGE

Spanish is the official language. English is widely spoken, especially in tourist areas. Traffic signs and most menus in restaurants are in Spanish, although menus in tourist regions tend to be multilingual.

| | | | |
|---|---|---|---|
| yes | *sí* | goodnight | *buenos noches* |
| no | *no* | excuse me | *perdóneme* |
| please | *por favor* | how are you? | *¿cómo está?* |
| thank you | *gracias* | do you speak | *¿habla usted* |
| you're welcome | *de nada* | English? | *inglés?* |
| hello | *hola* | I don't understand | *no entiendo* |
| goodbye | *adiós* | how much? | *¿cuánto?* |
| good morning | *buenos dias* | open/closed | *abierto/cerrar* |
| good afternoon | *buenos tardes* | where is…? | *¿dónde está…?* |
| | | | |
| single room | *cuarto sencillo* | room service | *servicio de* |
| double room | *cuarto doble* | | *habitaciones* |
| one night | *una noche* | bath | *baño* |
| reservation | *reserva* | shower | *ducha/regadera* |
| key | *llave* | toilet | *sanitario/baño* |
| | | | |
| bank | *banco* | banknote | *billete de nanco* |
| exchange office | *casa de cambio* | traveler's cheques | *cheque de viajero* |
| post office | *el correo* | credit card | *tarjeta de crédito* |
| coin | *moneda* | change | *suelto/dinero* |
| | | | |
| café/bar | *café/bar* | dessert | *postre* |
| table | *mesa* | bill | *la cuenta* |
| waiter/waitress | *camarero/camarera* | beer | *cerveza* |
| starter | *entrada* | wine | *vino* |
| main course | *plato principales* | water | *agua* |
| | | | |
| airport | *aeropuerto* | single ticket | *billete solo* |
| train | *ferrocarril* | return ticket | *de ida y vuelta* |
| bus | *autobus* | non-smoking | *prohibido fumar* |
| boat | *barco* | today | *hoy* |
| ticket | *boleto* | tomorrow | *mañana* |

# Best places to see

# 1 Altos de Chavón

**Stroll the cobbled streets and shop for paintings in this reconstructed medieval village perched high on cliffs above the Río Chavón.**

Altos de Chavón is open to everyone and demands at least half a day, or an evening. A replica 16th-century Mediterranean village complete with fountains and cobbled streets, it's more real than a movie set. It was built in 1976 by Dominican masons, carpenters and ironsmiths, under the direction of cinematographer Roberto Copa. Not simply a tourist attraction, it is a Cultural Center Foundation, a non-profit and educational institute,

that houses the School of Design and the Regional Museum of Archaeology.

The highlight is a full-size Greek amphitheater backed by 12 columns to represent the disciples of Christ. Frank Sinatra performed the first open-air concert here in 1982, followed by Julio Iglesias and Gloria Estefan. It's a bring-your-own-cushions event with tremendous acoustics. Around the village are quaint houses that are actually shops, complete with wooden shutters and climbing bougainvillea. There's a French bakery, restaurants, artists' studios, souvenirs, a craft center and the Chavón Art Gallery. By night the place is romantically lit by lamps and there are some good bars and classy restaurants.

The Museo Arqueológico has objects from the Taino Indian period and documents the Colombian legacy. The Church of St. Stanislaus, furnished with a statue of the Virgin Mary, is adorable and named after Poland's patron saint in honor of Pope John Paul II.

🕇 22J ✉ Near Casa de Campo Resort, La Romana ☎ 523 3333 (Casa de Campo Resort) 🕔 Various opening times for shops and attractions 👤 Free 🍴 French bakery and choice of bars, restaurants ($$–$$$) 🚌 Self-drive, or *gua-gua* or taxi from La Romana ❓ Regular music and concerts held

# 2 Bahía de Samaná

**A wild and dramatic peninsula visited annually by schools of magnificent humpback whales and a rare opportunity to see them close up.**

On a map you can see how the 30-mile (48-km) long Península de Samaná forms the famous Bahía de Samaná (Samana Bay) where, from January to March, the humpback whales *(Megaptera novaeangliae)* congregate to breed and rear their newborn calves.

It's estimated that up to 10,000 humpback whales visit the coastline of the Dominican Republic after spending the summer months in the polar region feeding grounds. What sets them apart from other whales is the way they breach from the water. The whale heaves out of the ocean on its side, twists in the air and crashes its 40 tons of flesh back down in a memorable display. Huge flippers, almost a third of the body length and measuring up to 16ft (5m), are often the last to slip beneath the waves.

Fortunately for us, the humpback whale swims close to the coast. You can spot them either by standing on the shore at Banco de la Plata, north of Puerto Plata, or by hopping aboard a whale-watching cruise (➤ 124) into the Bahía de Samaná. Day trips can also drop you off on the popular offshore island of Cayo Levantado (➤ 107), known for its gorgeous beach. The town of Sánta Barbara de Samaná itself dates from the mid-1700s when families from the Canary Islands set up home here. It is backed by the mountains of the Cordillera Samaná.

✚ 11D ✉ Península de Samaná ✋ Tours: moderate–expensive 🚌 Tour operators or bus from Santo Domingo and Puerto Plata
ℹ️ Edificio Gubernamental, Calle Santa Barbara, Samana
☎ 538 2332

# 3 Cordillera Central

**Lush tropical forests and coffee plantations rise to the pine-clad backbone of the Dominican Republic and the highest peaks in the Caribbean.**

Punching up through the heart of the country is the Cordillera Central, the "Dominican Alps." Connected to the Massif du Nord in Haiti, the range bends southwards until it meets the Caribbean coast and is the main watershed of the country. Visually, it's a world away from the beach. Walk or ride on horseback through forests to waterfalls or try rafting down the Río Yaque del Norte, the longest river in the country. See barefoot children astride mules fetching the daily water. It's a poor, simple life where locals scratch an existence from growing coconuts, bananas, avocados and coffee.

Over the past decade the Cordillera Central has attracted more visitors as

the country pushes adventure tourism as an alternative to the beach holiday. Hundreds of walkers tackle the 30-mile (48-km) ascent of Pico Duarte (10,414ft/3,175m), the highest peak, each year.

First climbed in 1944, the mountain bore the name Pico Trujillo after the country's ruthless dictator, Rafael Leonidas Trujillo, who added a few extra feet to its actual height in an elaborate boast. Following Trujillo's assassination in 1961, the mountain was renamed in honour of Juan Pablo Duarte, who fought for indepedence in 1844. Almost anyone can have a go at trekking to Pico Duarte on a three-day, two-night trek. Or do it the easy way and ride a pack mule. It is spectacular, with a beauty to rival the high forests of Nepal. The alpine aroma is sweet. Temperatures drop low enough, however, for sweaters, and some people have even reported snowflakes falling on the summit.

Farther south, in the Valle Nuevo, only the fit attempt the trek through an unspoiled forest. It involves days of walking and you need plenty of stamina.

✚ 3D–16J ✉ Parque Nacional Armando Bermúdez/Parque Nacional José del Carmen Ramirez ✋ Free 🍴 Bars and restaurants in Jarabacoa ($–$$) 🚌 Bus from Santo Domingo to Jarabacoa or tour operators: Iguana Mama ☎ 571 0908; www.iguanamama.com
ℹ National parks office ☎ 472 3717

# 4 Isla Saona

**Reached only by boat, the island boasts
pristine, white beaches shaded with
swinging palms and a shallow sea of blue
and green hues.**

Isla Saona is a jewel in the Parque Nacional del
Este (▶ 129), a trapezoid at the far southeastern
tip of the country. The park itself is known for its
beauty and impressive caves with pre-Columbian
petroglyphs and pictographs. Sightings of iguanas,
dolphins and turtles are common.

Saona was discovered by Christopher Columbus
and is believed to be named after Sabona in Italy. It
is the only inhabited place in the park. Reached only
by speedboat or catamaran, the island is a popular,
full-day trip. In fact, it's a welcome relief to leave
behind the sprawling resorts that appear to have
eaten up the south coast. You speed past a
shoreline of dry and sub-tropical humid forest still
thick, considering that 60 percent of the coconuts

were pulverized by Hurricane Georges in 1998. Starfish are magnified on the ocean floor and flying fish hover over the surface, racing with you, their fins flapping.

On a boat tour you usually arrive on the eastern side of Isla Saona, at a fishing village lined with pastel-colored, palm-wood houses. Souvenirs and paintings are sold here. From the village it takes a few minutes in the boat to reach the main beach. The perfect white sands are clean and there are no ostentatious hotels. There are flush toilets but they are about all that's modern. Langoustines and lobsters sizzle on hot plates at open-air eateries run by the tour operators. All you do is eat, sleep and snorkel.

✚ 22K–23L  ✉ Parque Nacional del Este, La Altagracia province  🐝 Moderate (included in boat tour)  🍴 Take a picnic, or book through an operator (lunch is included)
🚤 From La Romana or Bayahibe
ℹ National parks office  ☎ 472 3717

# 5 Lago Enriquillo

**Once crossed by the legendary Indian
chief and now a perfect spot to
photograph wild American crocodiles,
iguanas and flocks of pink flamingos.**

Lago Enriquillo is a remnant of an ancient channel
that united the Bay of Neiba in the Dominican
Republic with the Bay of Port-au-Prince in Haiti. The
lake is an inland saltwater sheet of tea-stain-colored
water and it lies 131ft (40m) below sea level, the
lowest point in the Caribbean. Over 300 American
crocodiles live here.

The lake is named after the Cacique Enriquillo, an
Indian chief who fought for freedom against the
Spaniards in this area. He utilized the island within
the lake, Isla Cabritos (➤ 143), as his retreat. No
human lives here nowadays, but there are plenty of
iguanas, the two species known as *rinoceros* and
*ricordi*. The iguanas and crocodiles are both
considered endangered and hunting is illegal.

You can take a tour just to the shores of the lake.
Here you'll definitely see iguanas. Because visitors
have fed them, they are now so tame that they

come running up to you like puppies. Groove lines in the sand indicate the drag of their tails. To see the crocodiles means a boat trip (➤ 144) across the lake to disembark at a small wooden jetty on Isla de Cabritos. Then it's a 1.5-mile (2.5-km) walk through a corridor of cacti to a beach made from minute shells. Go silently and you'll see crocodiles sunning on the banks, their mouths open to ventilate. As soon as they detect you they slide into the lake and swim away. The finale of the crocodile trip is a glide past pink flamingos before they take off en masse in amazing flight.

🕂 26Q ✉ Parque Nacional Isla Cabritos 🕔 Daily – permit required 🖐 Moderate 🍴 Drinks and snacks on site ($)
🚌 By tour operator or taxi from Baharona
ℹ National parks office ☎ 472 3717

# 6 Monumento a los Héroes, Santiago

**A legacy of extravagant dictatorship towers above Santiago de los Cabelleros, the country's second largest city.**

This eight-storey, 220ft-high (67m-high), white marble building is a monument to the nation's heroes of independence. To give it its full title, Monumento a los Héroes de la Restauración de la República pokes above the rooftops of the city known simply as Santiago. Built by Rafael Leonidas Trujillo, the egotistical dictator who ruled the country ruthlessly from 1930 to 1961, it is either grotesque or impressive – you decide. Trujillo had the habit of erecting monuments and busts in worship of himself wherever he found space.

Ornate, trimmed trees and national flags surround the bottom. Steps lead to the base, a cubic, mausoleum-style structure that rises to what resembles a screwdriver pointing upwards. Some say the figure at the top of the monument, which appears to be holding up the sky, was meant to be Trujillo. Inside, you can take the elevator or climb exhausting flights of stairs to the top, remembering your camera for the magnificent panoramic views of Santiago, bordered by mountains of the fertile Cibao Valley. At the top of the staircase are works by Spanish painter Vela Zanetti.

At sunset, watch the sun sink behind the mountains and the dust from the city streets puff up like clouds. Someone might try to sell you a rose, or potato chips. A bride and groom might be having their wedding photographs taken. On February 26, the day before the Independence Day celebrations, entire families gather together here. The children are dressed in colorful costumes speckled with tiny bells, and they wear carnival masks.

➕ 6C ✉ Santiago de los Caballeros 🕓 Open daily (times vary) 🖐 Inexpensive 🚌 Express bus from Santo Domingo or Puerto Plata

ℹ Ayuntamiento Municipal
☎ 582 5885

# 7 Parque Historico La Isabela

**The foundations of Columbus's first New World settlement teeter at the edge of the Atlantic, where archaeologists are still making discoveries.**

Christopher Columbus brought the Spanish language to the Dominican Republic. He was blown to the island he named *La Isla Española* accidentally, by trade winds. Columbus originally

landed in Haiti, in December 1492. There he ordered that the wrecked timber from his ship, *Santa María*, be used to build a fort called Puerta de la Navidad (Port Christmas). On his return voyage Columbus discovered the fort had been burned and his men massacred. He then founded La Isabela in honor of the Spanish queen. The area was divided into five territories, each headed by a Taino Indian chief. The Indians used stone cooking implements and were skilled at creating ceramics and carving images of their own gods from mahogany. The Spaniards enlisted the Indians to dig for gold but due to disease or fighting both natives and colonists began to die. You can see some of their graves, although the white crosses are not authentic.

In the Parque Historico La Isabela (La Isabela Historic Park) a fraction of the walls of Columbus's castle are visible, as are the foundations of the first church of the New World and the fortress. It's difficult to distinguish what is original and what was rebuilt for the 500th anniversary celebrations of Columbus's discovery. A museum displays Indian objects, from necklaces to carvings of turtle shells and arrowheads. There's a drawing of Columbus, a model of the *Santa María* and, outside, a reconstructed Taino Indian settlement.

✚ 4A ✉ Bay of La Isabela, south of El Castillo town ⏰ 8–5:30 ✋ Inexpensive 🚌 Best reached by tour or self-drive
ℹ National parks office ☎ 472 3717

# 8 Punta Cana

**Punta Cana is a sight to behold – a knuckle of land on the east coast made up of sands as white as sugar stretching to the Caribbean Sea.**

Basically, when people come to Punta Cana, it's usually for the top attraction; 31 miles (50km) of blissful beach lapped by sea streaked with iridescent ribbons of turquoise, sky blue and green, all fired up at the end of the day by a brilliant orange sunset. It is romantic and relaxing, and a place to recharge (apparently, Bill and Hillary Clinton came here to rest after leaving the White House). Singer Julio Iglesias and Dominican-born fashion designer Oscar de la Renta have properties here and are co-developers of the Punta Cana Resort, a luxurious retreat with a flower-shaped pool yards from a talcum-powder white beach with swaying palms.

The destination itself, "Punta Cana" is loosely used to describe the pockets of Juanillo, Punta Cana, Cabeza de Toro, Bávaro, El Cortecito, Macao and Uvero Alto, where a string of around 30 ultra all-inclusive resorts have sprung up. Unless touring the country by road, or arriving by private yacht, holidaymakers fly into Punta Cana's own international airport, topped with a grass-thatched roof. Runways are big enough to accommodate Boeing 747s.

From your resort you can book ecological walks through tropical jungle, take 4x4 motorbike adventure tours or a boat trip out to Isla Saona

(➤ 42) and the Parque Nacional del Este (➤ 129). You can go horseback-riding, sailing and take part in or watch the summer big game fishing tournaments. If you like golf, Punta Cana offers three world-class 18-hole courses, with more on the drawing board.

✚ 24J 🚌 Express bus from Santo Domingo ✖ Punta Cana, Higüey

# 9 Puerto Plata

**The place Columbus named the "port of silver" and its statue-crowned peak gives you cigars, amber jewelry and shopping bargains galore.**

Those that make the effort to visit Puerto Plata, the largest town on the north coast, are in for a treat. It's easily explored on foot. The pretty square of Parque Luperón is the focal point, surrounded by pastel-painted 19th-century architecture and the art deco-style Catholic Church of San Felipe. Sit in the square beside the central pavilion and listen as the clock tower passes the time. On Sunday mornings you'll hear harmonious celebrations at the white-painted church on the corner. The *malecón* (seafront promenade) comes alive at festival time. You can't miss the brass statue of General Gregorio Luperón, pointing towards the city. He fought against the Spanish in the mid-1800s and, when in power, briefly made Puerto Plata the republic's capital.

Puerto Plata is so called because Columbus either thought the harbor shimmered like a silver plate or the backdrop of mountains shone like the precious metal. He introduced sugarcane, which became as important as the port's trade in tobacco and cattle hides. The port was abandoned when its economy was undermined by locals trading with enemy pirate fleets. The fort, bristling with cannons, was built at the mouth of the bay to ward off pirates. It's well-preserved and ringed with a grassy bank.

➕ 6B 🚌 Express bus from Santo Domingo, *gua-gua* or taxi from the north coast

ℹ Calle Hermanas Mirabal 8 ☎ 586 3676

# 10 Zona Colonial, Santo Domingo

**First European city in the New World and seat of Spanish power, this historic gathering of architecture and treasures is now world renowned.**

It's easy to see why Zona Colonial, in the capital of Santo Domingo, was declared a World Heritage Site by UNESCO in 1990. Once ruled by Spain in the days of pirates, galleons and gold, its late-Gothic style architecture bears a hint of Renaissance and years of wear are traceable on rusty cannons. See how the people lived at that time at the home of Columbus's son, Diego, now

the Museo Alcázar de Colón (➤ 89). The Catedral
Basílica Menor de Santa Maria, Primada de
América (➤ 85), with its early motifs of
Catholicism, is claimed by Dominicans to be the
first cathedral of the Americas. Cobbled Las Damas
street is said to be the first street. Then there's the
first university, the first hospital... the list goes on.

Splendid though it is,
Santo Domingo was
built in 1498 with
enormous cost to the
lives of native Indian
and African slaves.
Columbus's brother,
Bartolomé, built it like a
fortress on the eastern
side of the Río Ozama to protect the people from
pirates. After being destroyed by a hurricane it was
moved to its present site.

So contained in a grid is Zona Colonial that all its
sites can be seen in a full day's stroll (but take
longer if you're really interested). Be wary of
unofficial tour guides. If in doubt, ask to see their
government-issued card. To absorb the atmosphere
and learn a bit of colonial history, it's best to stay
overnight and sample the old city's cafés and bistros.

➕ *Santo Domingo 5c* 🚌 Express buses from major towns
ℹ️ 103 Calle Isabel la Católica, Parque Colón ☎ 686 3858
🕐 Daily 9–5

# Best things to do

# Great places to have lunch

### ❖❖El Concon Restaurante ($$)

An open-air venue for authentic Italian food, including oven-baked pizzas, meats on wood-fired grill and pastas.

✉ Avenida Boulevard, Juan Dolio ☎ 526 2652 🕒 Daily 11–11

### ❖❖Le Flamboyan ($$)

Dominican-style restaurant with a palm thatched roof, with frequent live music evenings. Lobster, mussels and conch, soups and meats grilled over a wood fire.

✉ Playa El Cortecito, Bávaro ☎ 552 0639 🕒 Daily 11am–midnight

### Hemingway's Café ($)

Live bands perform in this popular meeting place The food is a familiar mix of burgers, burritos, tacos, nachos, steaks and pasta.

✉ Playa Dorada Plaza ☎ 320 2230 🕒 Daily 11am–2am

### Neptuno's Club ($$$)

Exquisite setting over a lagoon. Good fish and shellfish.

✉ Calle Duarte 12, Boca Chica ☎ 523 4703 ⏰ Daily 9am–11pm, midnight at weekends

### ♦♦El Patio ($)

French-Spanish inspired choice of meats and some fish.

✉ Las Mercedes, Zona Colonial, Santo Domingo ☎ 685 9331
⏰ Daily 7am–midnight

### ♦♦Pat'e Palo Brasserie ($–$$)

Pirate-themed restarant serving excellent salads, Mexican beans, fish, steak and pasta.

✉ Atarazana 25, Zona Colonial, Santo Domingo ☎ 687 8089
⏰ Mon–Thu 11:30am–12;30am, Fri–Sun 11:30am–1:30am

### ♦♦♦Reina de Espana ($$$)

Dominican specialties, and also Spanish, Italian and French.

✉ Cervantes/Santiago streets, near Malecon ☎ 685 2588

### ♦♦♦Restaurant Don Pepe ($–$$)

Seafood, meats and local Dominican specialties.

✉ Avenida Pasteur 41 ☎ 686 8481

### ♦♦Samurai ($$)

Great value for money Japanese restaurant complete with sushi bar and tatami table seating. Extensive choice.

✉ Avenida Abraham Lincoln ☎ 565 1621 ⏰ Daily noon–midnight

### ♦♦Starei ($$)

Creole and shellfish specialties, within the beautiful Altos de Chavón (► 36–37). A gorgeous romantic setting.

✉ Altos de Chavón, La Romana ☎ 523 3333 ⏰ Daily 11–11

# Best golf courses

## SANTO DOMINGO

### Las Lagunas Country Club
The course is based on a Peter Dye design, set in verdant tropical countryside. 18 holes, par 72.
✉ 20 Duarte Highway ☎ 372 7441

### Santo Domingo Country Club
Opened in 1920 but more recently enhanced by a Robert Trent Jones course among gently sloping hills. 18 holes, par 72.
✉ Calle Isabel Aguiar ☎ 530 6606

## AROUND THE COUNTRY

### Dye Forc
Opened in 2003, 18 holes, par 72. The course runs parallel with the Chavón river.
✉ Casa de Campo, La Romano ☎ 523 3333; www.casadecampo.com

### Guavaberry Golf Club
Gary Player designed 18 hole course with the challenging 15th nicknamed "Island Hole".
✉ Costa Caribe Resort, Juan Dolio ☎ 333 4653

### The Links
Casa de Campo's second championship course. 18 holes, par 72.
✉ Casa de Campo, La Romana ☎ 523 3333; www.casadecampo.com

### Los Marlins Golf Course
Near Juan Dolio beach. 18 holes, par 72.
✉ Metro Country Club, Las Américas Highway, Juan Dolio ☎ 526 3315

### Playa Dorada Golf Course
Exceptional greens and pleasant lagoon setting. 18 holes, par 72.
✉ Playa Dorada, Puerto Plata ☎ 320 3472; www.playadoradagolf.com

### Playa Grande Golf Course
Ten holes that overlook the Caribbean Sea. Exclusive resort.
18 holes, par 72.
✉ Km 6 Carretera Río San Juan–Cabrera ☎ 582 0860

### Punta Cana Golf Course
Peter B. Dye's latest challenge course with views of the Caribbean
coastline. 18 holes.
✉ Punta Cana ☎ 959 4653; www.puntacana.com

### The Teeth of the Dog
World-renowned championship course set on the edge of the
Caribbean coastline. 18 holes, par 72.
✉ Casa de Campo, La Romana ☎ 523 3333; www.casadecampo.com

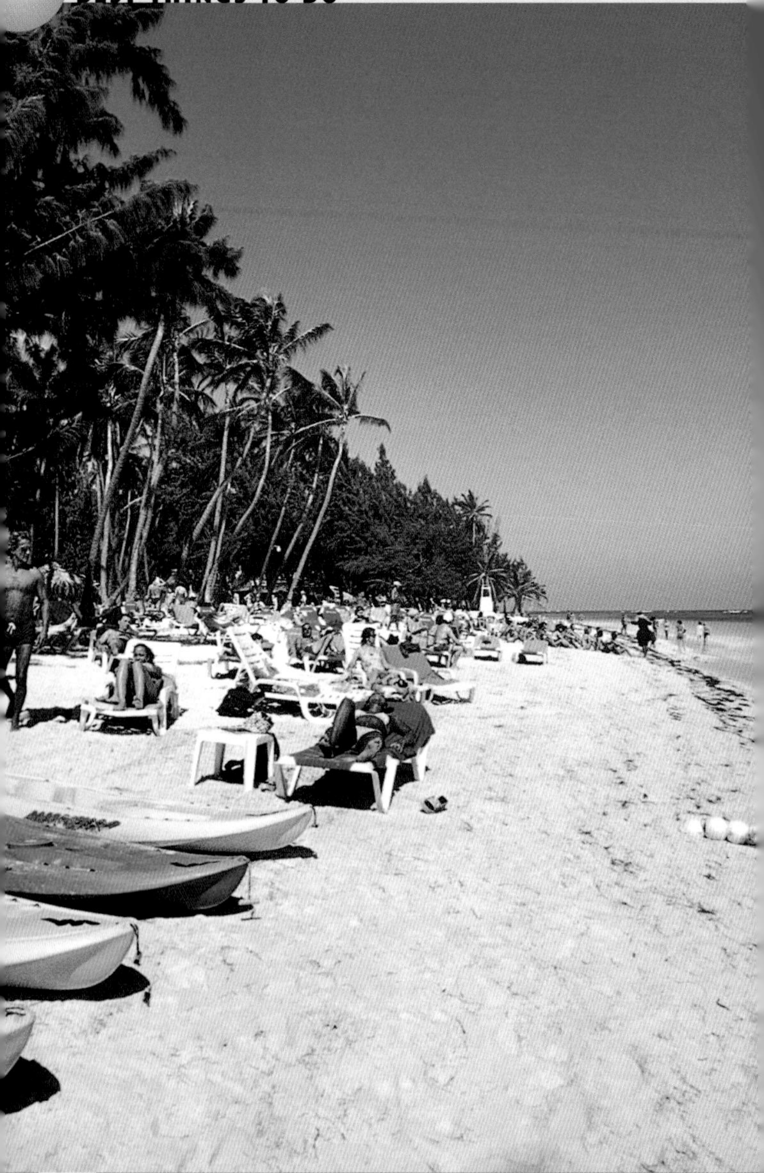

# Great beaches

### Cabarete
A lively resort, famed for its windsurfing (► 106).

### Sosúa
A well-visited stretch of beach, as bustling as Cabarete (► 118).

### Playa Dorada
The beach of **Puerto Plata**, a caramel curve of sand with rock pools where children can search for crabs (► 52).

### Playa Boca Chica
This sheltered lagoon makes it ideal for children (► 133).

### Punta Cana
The kind of soft, white sand beach known as paradise. Good water sports (► 50).

### Cayo Levantado
Setting of a Bacardi drinks television commercial(► 107).

### Isla Saona
A picture perfect mix of crystal waters, aquamarine colors and white, powdery sand (► 42).

### Bayahibe
A young person's hangout, busy with cruisers to Isla Saona (► 127).

### Playa Grande
A northern water sports mecca (► 115).

### Playa Rincon
A beach still left to the forces of nature.

# Wildlife watching

There's a wealth of wildlife in the Dominican Republic so make sure you look for these creatures:

**Hispanolan parakeets** flit around Parque Nacional Los Haïtises (➤ 110) and in the Cordillera Central (➤ 40).

**Manatees** are spotted in the Parque Nacional del Este (➤ 129), around Isla Saona (➤ 42), and at the Nacional Parque Monte Cristi (➤ 114).

**Humpback whales** visit the Península de Samaná each winter to calve (➤ 38).

**American crocodiles** can be seen basking in the sun or lurking in the still waters of Lago Enriquillo (➤ 44).

**Iguanas** are so tame on Isla Cabritos they run up to you expecting a tidbit (➤ 143).

**Dolphins** frolic in the seas and oceans around the Dominican Republic.

**Pink flamingos** launch themselves from the shores of Lago Enriquillo (➤ 44).

**Sea lions** make the audience laugh at Manatí Park (➤ 72).

**Sea turtles** crawl onto many patches of sand to lay their eggs. Also at the Acuarío Nacional in Santo Domingo (➤ 84).

**American kestrels** inhabit some of the the national parks but are hard to spot, they also perch on the top of telephone poles around Puerto Plata in the north (➤ 52).

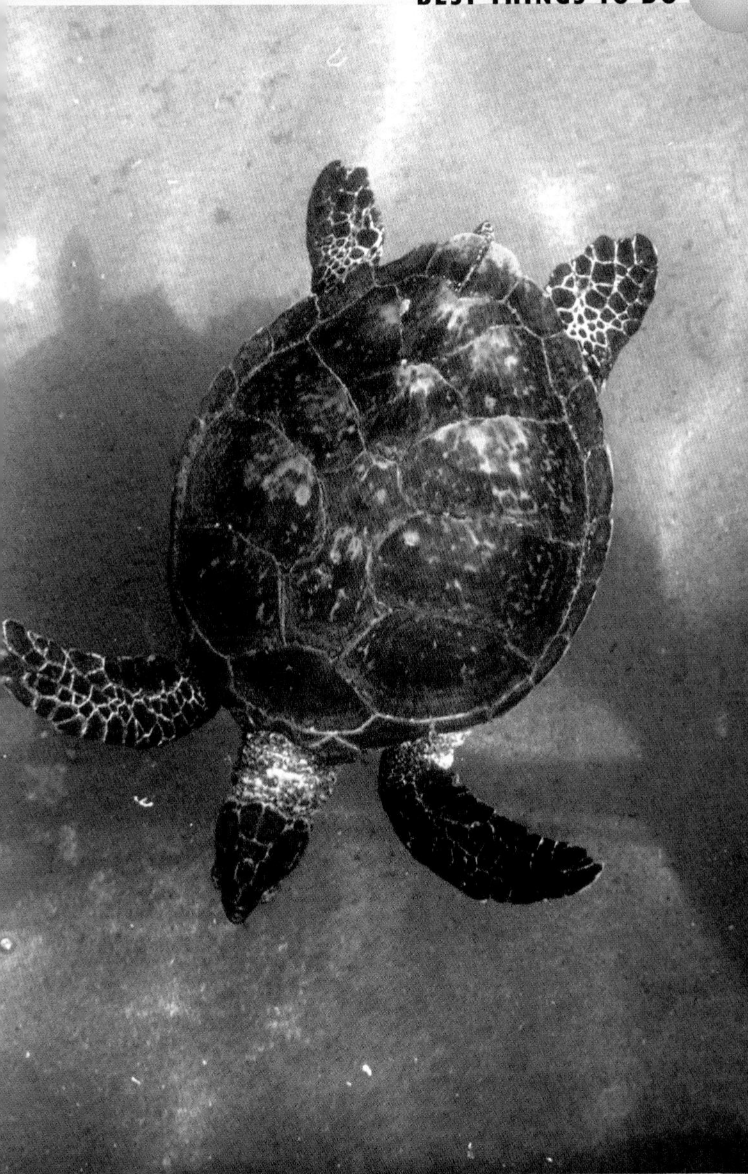

# Top activities

**Stroll the beaches** of Playa Dorada on the "Amber Coast"
(► 115).

**Go on safari** into the mountainous interior (➤ 154).

**Photograph waterfalls** in the Dominican Alps, the Salto de Jimenoa at Jarabacoa being the most impressive (➤ 146).

**Tour the Zona Colonial**, the historic old city of the capital Santo Domingo (➤ 54).

**Go birdwatching** in Parque Nacional Los Haïtses on an organized adventure tour (➤ 110).

**Learn to windsurf** at Cabarete, the world-famous championship resort (➤ 106).

**Play golf** at one of many courses, some offering superb landscaping and design (➤ 60).

**Learn to scuba dive/snorkel** with recognized diving schools, then book dives to the coral reefs and spectacular wrecks (➤ 132).

**Watch baseball** at the stadia in Santo Domingo.

**Go rafting** on the Río Yaque del Norte, the country's longest river.

**Merengue** the evening away at a local fiesta.

**Trek** the forests on horseback.

# Stunning views

● Plaza Espana in the Colonial Zone: in the footsteps of Columbus (➤ 54).

● Along the thronging Malecón in Santo Domingo.

● Isla Cabritos with its tame iguanas (➤ 143).

● The myriad species of the submarine environment at Cayo Paraiso.

● From the summit of Pico Isabel de Torres (➤ 114).

● The laid-back life on Bozo Beach, Cabarete (➤ 106).

● The lush mangroves of Los Haïtises (➤ 68).

● "Robinson Crusoe" desert island views on Isla Saona (➤ 42).

● Whales breaking the surface at Samana Bay (➤ 38).

# a walk around Puerto Plata

**Although some of Puerto Plata's 100,000 inhabitants still work in the sugarcane trade and agriculture, many more now work in tourism and supporting services at resorts along the north coast.**

At the start point, Parque Luperón (➤ 110), you can bargain with a guide who will show you the sights. Some are very knowledgeable on the history and this is their only form of work. Prices can be reasonable. Alternatively do-it-yourself around this compact place. Before you start, admire the Glorieta Sicilian pavilion and visit the Catedral de San Felipe.

*Cross over to the white church on the corner with Calle Beller. If it's Sunday morning, you might hear Mass and*

*hymn singing. Head back towards the cathedral
and turn right down Calle Duarte.*

Notice the Victorian gingerbread decoration on
the houses and ornate verandas. Note too, how
chunks of this architecture have been knocked
down to make way for something modern and
concrete.The Museo de Ambar Dominicano
(Dominican Amber Museum) (➤ 109) is easy to
detect. Spot the red and black *Jurassic Park* logos
on a pure white building.

*Retrace your steps back towards the cathedral
and square, but turn right and continue all the
way up Separación until the street meets with Av.
Gregorio Luperón, the malecón by the oceanfront.
Enjoy the views before turning left towards the Fuerte
de San Felipe (➤ 106).*

Around the base of the fort walls are hawkers selling
souvenirs.

*From here head back to the square along José del
Carmen Ariza for some serious souvenir shopping down
the main thoroughfares of Calle Beller and Calle Duarte.*

**Distance** Around
1 mile (2km)
**Time** Half a day
**Start/end point**
Parque Luperón

# Places to take the children

**Manati Park** animal exhibits and shows.
✉ Ctra Manati, Bavaro/Higüey Highway, Bavaro ☎ 221 9444

**Oceanworld Adventures** the largest marine park in the Caribbean (Puerto Plata).
✉ Playa Confresi, Puerto Plata
☎ 291 1000; www.oceanworld.net
🕐 Daily 9–6

**Parque Zoologique Nacional** with collections of native animals.
✉ Avenida Los Arroyos de Arroyo Hondo, Santo Domingo ☎ 562 3149
🕐 Tue–Sun 9–5

**Dolphin Island Park** where you can swim with the dolphins.
✉ Ctra Manati, Bavaro/Higüey Highway, Bavaro ☎ 221 9444

**Acuario Nacional** with its underwater plexi-glass tunnel.
✉ Avenida 28 de Enero, Santo Domingo ☎ 7661709 🕐 Tue–Sun 9:30–5:30

**On a pony trek** to enjoy some beautiful scenery.

**Whale watching** at Samana Bay (► 38).

**To Lago Enriquillo** to see wild crocodiles (► 44).

**Off-road on a safari** for some thrilling adventure.

**Snorkelling** anywhere in the shallows to find incredible tropical fish.

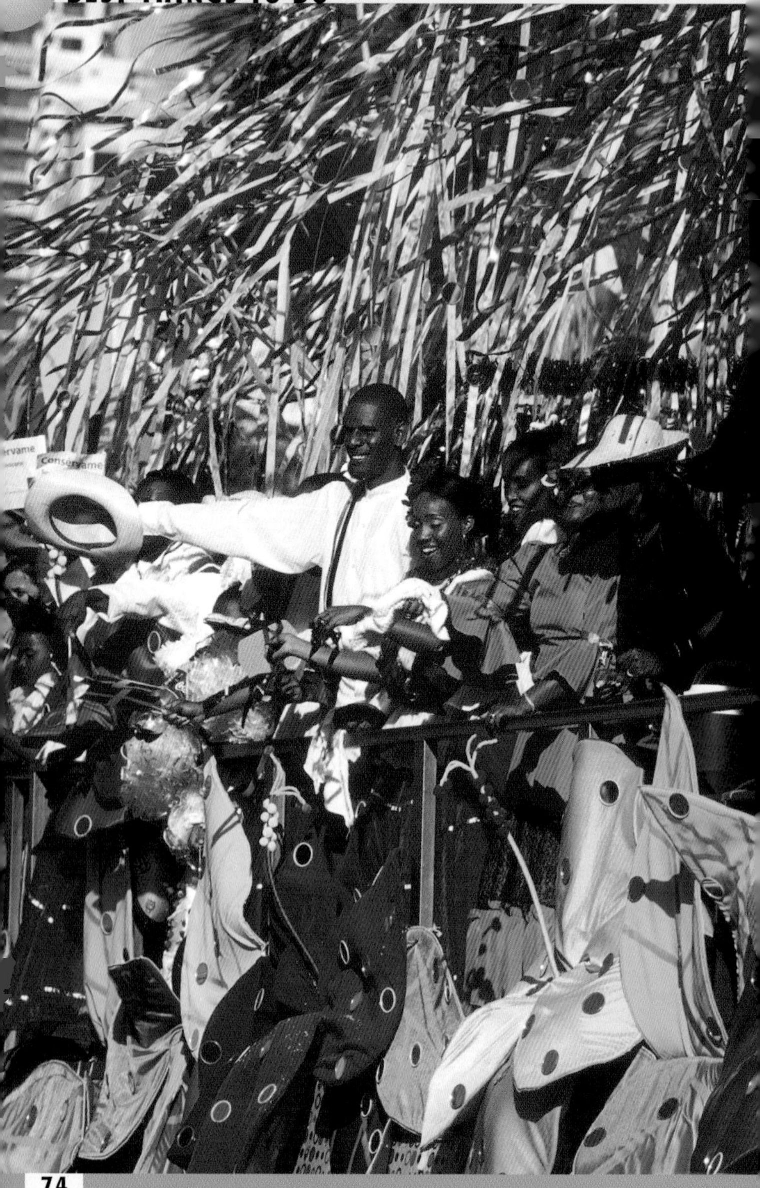
Conservame

# Festivals and fiestas

### Carnival
Every Sunday in February is a day to party in this nationwide celebration where Dominicans don colorful outfts and run round hitting each other over the head with pigs' bladders!

### Independence Day
A nationwide celebration on 27th February, the highlight of which is the parade in Santo Domingo.

### Semana Santa (Holy week celebrations)
Celebrated throughout the Dominican Republic, the Christian festivities coincide with a voodoo celebration, making for a colorful festival of parades and processions.

### Puerto Plata cultural festival
During the first week in June you'll find the *malecón* teeming with musicians and entertainment, while around Parque Central there are displays and stalls for arts and crafts.

### Cabarete race week
Kitesurfers and windsurfers compete at the Playa Encuentro, west of Cabarete.

### Merengue festival
As the country's favourite music it seems only fair to celebrate it twice. Starting in the third week in July, you'll find the *malecón* in Santo Domingo and Boca Chica packed with dancers every night for the duration of the two week festival. A similar festival in held the third week in June in Puerto Plata.

### Jazz festival
During the first week in October Sosúa and Cabarete host an annual jazz festival that attracts an international line-up.

# Shopping and souvenirs

**WHAT TO BUY**
**Amber and Larimar** – natural minerals and rocks sold loose or made into incredible jewelry.

**Paintings** – vibrant artwork from the Dominican Republic and Haiti.

**Cigars** – some of the finest hand-rolled smokes in the world.

**Rum** – the fiery drink that fires the Dominican spirit.

**Merengue music** – to relive the memory at home.

**Pieces of Eight** – real coins recovered from Spanish shipwrecks.

**WHERE TO BUY**
**Zona Colonial Santo Domingo** (➤ 54) – with shops housed in majestic historic stone buildings.

Main Street **Cabarete** (➤ 106) – rows of shops selling kitsch souvenirs and tropical clothing.

The art galleries of **Las Terrenas** (➤ 119) – for great original art.

The smart boutiques of **Playa Dorada Plaza** (➤ 123) – high-class merchandise in modern tropical surroundings.

# Best places to stay

### Hotel Gran Bahia Principe Cayacoa ($$$)

Set on a dramatic headland overlooking a majestic stretch of sand, the Cayacoa offers 295 rooms and suites situated in series of six storey low-rise towers or in smaller villas surrounded by tropical woodland. Rooms have rosewood and rattan furnishings, each with a balcony. Sea-facing rooms have exceptional views over the beach or coves. There are four restaurants and three bars to choose from. There's a lift linking the hotel with the main beach below and the famous "road to nowhere" links to two offshore islets.

✉ Loma Puerto Escondido, Samana ☎ 538 3135; www.bahia-principe.com

### ❤❤Hotel Todo Blanco ($-$$)

The Todo Blanco makes a great place to chill out. A whitewashed colonial style mansion houses the standard rooms with their generous balconies or patios and this main building is flanked by eight beachfront rooms. Room décor in "tropical minimalist" but the communal areas, including the bar and restaurant have an "out of Africa" feel with their rattan furniture and wooden slatted shutters. The palm-filled gardens lead directly onto the waterfront. Ideal for a romantic escape or some serious R&R.

✉ Las Galeras ☎ 538 0201; www.hoteltodoblanco.com

### ❤❤La Palmas Residence ($$)

This small villa resort is an excellent alternative to the big hotels for those who want a more peaceful and intimate family holiday with the opportunity to self cater. Twenty-three, two-bedroomed villas are set in a tropical garden, each with a comfortable lounge, kitchen with refrigerator and cooker and terrace plus an outside grill for barbeques. The resort is 164ft (50m) from a lovely stretch of sand with warm shallow water and a ten-minute walk from the centre of Las Terrenas.

✉ Avenida Benelux, Las Terrenas ☎ 240 6436; www.vamosalaspalmas.com

### ☗☗☗Punta Cana Resort ($$)

Set on a naturally superb white beach and renowned for its attention to detail, service and food. Ocean-view rooms and new luxury golf villas with interiors designed by Dominican fashion designer, Oscar de la Renta, each with own private beach, and some with open-air hot tubs. Golf course designed by Pete Dye. Good diving and snorkeling and trips to a national park.

✉ Higüey, Punta Cana ☎ 221 2262/687 8745; www.puntacana.com

### The Sivory Punta Cana ($$$)

A high-class hideaway, The Sivory is a member of the Small Luxury Hotels of the World. The tropical styling takes more than a passing influence from South East Asia.

The hotel serves "Art Cuisine" at its three gourmet restaurants and you can explore the cellar with its 8,000 bottles of wine. The suites-only property starts with junior suites with a two-person tub. Enjoy the huge palm shaded pool or take treatments in the bijou spa.

✉ Sivory Beach, Punta Cana ☎ 552 0500; www.sivorypuntacana.com

### ☗☗☗Sofitel Frances Santo Domingo ($$–$$$)

A very prestigious hotel housed in a 16th-century colonial mansion in the heart of the Zona Colonial. Top-class restaurant serving French cuisine, plus bar and relaxation areas. A lovely hotel for sightseeing and touring the historic quarter and museums.

✉ Calle Las Mercedes, Esq Arzobispo Meriño, Zona Colonial ☎ 685 9331; www.sofitel.com

# Exploring

Palm-lined beaches, engulfed by aquamarine waters and backed by fertile tropical vegetation, first tempted the gold-seeking explorer, Christopher Columbus, to set foot upon the Dominican Republic's shores.

These days tourists arrive to pulsating *merengue* music before being whisked off to all-inclusive resorts and hotels along developed coastlines. The Dominican Republic has much more to offer than just resort-based holidays. From tropical rainforest and mountains to desert-dry savannah dotted with cacti, the natural landscape of the country is amazingly diverse. It's impossible, even during a two-week stay, to see everything. Tours are plentiful, though, and venturing outside your hotel complex or resort to explore or have lunch by the roadside means you'll be more in touch with the country and its people.

# Santo Domingo

Santo Domingo

**Originally called Nueva Isabela, Santo Domingo was founded in 1498 by Columbus's brother, Bartolomé, on the eastern bank of the river, Río Ozama. Destroyed by a hurricane, the city was moved in 1502 to its present site and governed by Columbus's son, Diego. The name is thought to be derived from the 12th-century teaching apostle, Santo Domingo de Guzman, inventor of the rosary. During his dictatorship Trujillo renamed the capital Ciudad Trujillo in honor of himself, although it reverted back to Santo Domingo after his assassination in 1961.**

Numerous hurricanes have left their mark so what you see is a mix of layers and add-ons, with some old colonial buildings restored by well-known hotel groups. For daytrippers there are shops, boutiques, an immaculate botanic garden, art galleries, museums and an aquarium. A new swing bridge across the river takes you to the east, to a monument (said to contain the remains of Columbus), the aquarium and beaches enjoyed by the locals.

Time your visit to Santo Domingo on Independence Day, February 27 (or the last Sunday in February – check beforehand) to witness either the patriotism of the Dominican rulers or their extended egos. The nation's fighting force – troops, commandos, marines and the police riot squad – stand to attention in the blistering heat. They then march past the president and his generals on the main ocean-front artery, Avenida George Washington. The parade ends with a posse of big guns, tanks and fighter planes before four parachutists land at the president's feet.

## ACUARÍO NACIONAL

The National Aquarium has an attractive landscaped setting alongside the blue of the Caribbean Sea. The marine animals and fish themselves are housed in tanks and scores of families are attracted to this, the largest aquarium in the Caribbean. You'll see plenty of sharks and turtles and the colorful fish and crustaceans (such as crab and shrimp) commonly found in Dominican waters.

🚹 18J ✉ Ave 28 de Enero ☎ 766 1709 (office hours Mon–Fri) 🕐 Guided tours only Tue–Sun 9:30–5:30 👋 Inexpensive 🍴 Kiosk serving drinks ($)

## ALTAR DE LA PATRIA

The pedestrianized El Conde, a favorite shopping haunt for Dominicans, has been transformed for tourists, with gift shops and cigar sellers. As you pass under the gate of Puerte El Conde, the white mausoleum, Altar de la Patria (Altar of the Nation), confronts you. Inside are the remains of the three heroes of independence: Juan Pablo Duarte, Francisco del Rosario Sánchez and Ramón Matías Mella. An eternal flame burns in a crypt below.

🚹 *Santo Domingo 4c* ✉ Parque Independencia, Zona Colonial 🕐 Daily 👋 Free 🍴 Along El Conde street ($–$$)

## CATEDRAL BASÍLICA MENOR DE SANTA MARIE, PRIMADA DE AMÉRICA

On the north side of the Parque Colón stands the most important monument in the country, the Catedral Basílica Menor de Santa Marie, Primada de América (first cathedral of the Americas). In the early 1500s Diego Columbus, Christopher's son, laid the first stone where a wooden church once stood. Construction took around 40 years, but the sculptor died before it was finished. This explains the lack of a proper bell tower and the mixture of architectural styles – a commanding blend of Gothic, Romanesque and baroque. Inside, under a magnificent vaulted ceiling are 14 chapels. Francis Drake sacked much of the cathedral and even slept in the Capilla de Santa Ana. It is believed that the sarcophagus containing the remains of Columbus was found here during restoration work in 1877. In 1992 the remains were moved for the 500th anniversary of Columbus's landing, to the Faro a Colón (► 87).

🕇 *Santo Domingo 6c* ✉ Parque Colón, Zona Colonial ☎ 682 3848 🕓 Daily 9–4 ✋ Free ❓ Dress appropriately, shorts and vests (tank-tops) not allowed

## FARO A COLÓN

Across the Río Ozamo, the Faro a Colón (Lighthouse to Columbus) is a colossal monument to the Spanish explorer, Christopher Columbus. It is a must to stop and look inside this blatant result of President Balaguer's extravagance. Built to house the supposed remains of Christopher Columbus, the lighthouse cost US$200 million. Its trademark is a string of rooftop lasers that project an image of a cross, visible for miles, onto the night sky. The winner of an architectural contest to design the monument was a British man, Joseph Gleve. He only managed to see the base being made because dictator Trujillo stopped construction, probably for economic reasons. Gleve died in 1965 and another designer worked on the monument until it was completed in 1991, ready for the 500th anniversary of Columbus's landing.

When visiting the monument, first you climb steps to an entrance decorated by marble tablets inscribed with quotations about exploration from the New Testament and from Greek philosophers. An alleyway down the center of the cross is flanked by mahogany doors, behind which are displays of objects representative of 65 countries. The marble mausoleum, guarded by the militia, purportedly contained the remains of Christopher Columbus, and is decorated with bronze and gold. Spain, Italy and Cuba also claim the remains of Columbus, and DNA tests begun by the University of Grenada in Spain in 2003 proved that the bones held in Spain matched that of the Columbus line. Tantalizingly, however, the study also concluded that the remains did not constitute a whole body, adding weight to the theory that parts of the explorer were interred in a number of cities in the old and new world. Originally housed in the cathedral ( ► 85) the structure was dismantled into hundreds of pieces and reassembled at its present site. The lighthouse is designed in such a way that the tomb is protected from hurricanes and earthquakes.

➕ *Santo Domingo 8b* ✉ Avenida Boulevard del Faro, Villa Duarte
☎ 591 1492 🕐 Tue–Sun 9–7 🍴 Inexpensive

## FORTALEZA OZAMA

Fortaleza Ozama (Fortress of Ozama) is considered the oldest of its type in the Americas. It was built from 1505 by Governor Nicolás de Ovando when the city was moved to this side of the river. An elaborate gateway welcomes you into an expanse of trim, green lawn stretching to the Torre del Homenaje (Tower of Homage). The tower resembles a medieval castle, with turrets and battlements. During

the many occupations of the country, the Spanish, French, Haitians and Americans flew their flag atop its battlements. Staircases lead to the top and to a grand view of the river and its traffic. In the grounds is a bronze statue of Gonzalo Fernández de Oviedo. Other details to look for around the fort are cannons pointing out across the river, coats of arms, the arsenal and the old army barracks.

➕ *Santo Domingo 6c* ✉ Calle de las Damas, Zona Colonial ☎ 685 8532
🕐 Daily 9–5 💶 Inexpensive ❓ Guided tours available

## MUSEO ALCÁZAR DE COLÓN

Diego Columbus's palace and Spanish seat of government is now the Museo Alcázar de Colón (House of Columbus). It was built by 300 Indian slaves from 1511 to 1516. Diego lived here with his wife, Doña María de Toledo, until 1523, when they returned to Spain. Here many expeditions to conquer more of the Americas were planned. Alcázar is an Arabic word and Moorish influences on the decorated beamed ceilings of the interior are noticeable. Carved mahogany details and candle holders sporting grotesque faces are said to ward off evil spirits. Few pieces of furniture are originals, though many are representative of that period or slightly later. Of particular interest is a replica of Diego's mahogany and gold-leaf bed, a writing bureau, a bed engraved with the Columbus family crest and a trunk made from African elephant hide. The English-speaking guide insists that the testament signed by Queen Isabella of Spain, giving power to Diego, is the real thing. The balcony overlooks the Plaza de la Hispanidad and the ruins of the Monasterio de San Francisco.

➕ *Santo Domingo 6b* ✉ Plaza España ☎ 682 4750 🕐 Tue–Sat 9–5, Sun 9–4 ✋ Inexpensive ❓ English-speaking guides offer tours

# a walk around Zona Colonial

This tour begins with the Catedral Primada de América (➤ 85) and Parque Colón (➤ 96) before exploring highlights of the old city.

*Head along El Conde Street and turn right at Calle Hostos. Walk further, passing attractive painted colonial buildings with wrought ironwork for windows, some of which are art galleries and cafés.*

The pink building, now the Italian Embassy, offers Dominicans Italian language and painting classes. Browse round the Ruinas del Hospital San Nicolás de Bari (➤ 98).

*Walk uphill, passing wooden houses on your left.*

The houses survived a hurricane in the 1930s. Immediately ahead are the ruins of the first monastery, Monasterio de San Francisco where, nowadays, Dominicans can marry.

*Turn downhill to busy Calle Arzobispo Meriño. Turn left and to the Museo Mundo de Ambar (➤ 95) on your left. Turn right out of the museum, cross the road and turn immediately left downhill and right into Plaza de la Hispanidad.*

Explore the Museo Alcázar de Colón (➤ 89).

*Walk alongside the river to Museo de las Casas Reales (► 93) on the right. Keep straight ahead, following Calle Las Damas, passing the Panteón Nacional (► 96) on the right, gift shops and the French Embassy. Eventually a side street on the left leads to the archway of the Fortaleza Ozama (► 88). Explore the fortress and battlements. Head back out of the archway and up Calle Pellerano Alfau until you face the cathedral and Parque Colón to the right.*

**Distance** 2 miles (3km)
**Time** Half a day with lunch, longer with shopping and rest stops. To see all the sites takes more than a day
**Start/end point** Parque Colón, Zona Colonial ✠ *Santo Domingo 6c*
**Lunch** Choice of restaurants at Plaza La Hispanidad ($–$$)

## MUSEO DE LAS ATARAZANAS

The atmospheric Museo de las Atarazanas (Shipyard or Maritime Museum) is housed in a former warehouse facing east over the Río Ozama. This maritime archaeological museum recounts life on a Spanish galleon for crew and passengers in the 17th century. More enthralling is the tale of the *Concepción*, part of the New World fleet which sank during a hurricane in 1641 on its way back to Spain. An expedition in 1686 did recover some silver and bullion. Nearly 300 years later, in 1976, Burt Webber and Jack Hoskins found 13 wrecks but not the *Concepción*. In 1978 a second, better equipped, expedition finally found the galleon, with a hoard of undiscovered treasure. At the time of writing the museum was closed for renovations that were due to be completed in 2007, however, Las Atarazanas area itself has undergone restoration and has now become popular for its boutiques and restaurants.

✚ *Santo Domingo 6b* ✉ Calle Colón No 4 La Atarazana, Zona Colonial
☎ 682 5834 ⊕ Closed for renovations, call for details ✋ Inexpensive

## MUSEO DE LAS CASAS REALES

The Museo La Casas Reales (Museum of the Royal Houses) occupies what was the 16th palace of the Spanish Governor's Royal Court. To its side is Calle Las Damas, the cobbled street of the ladies and the first street in the Americas. Nearly all the information signs in this brilliant museum are in Spanish, but you can rent a guide inside for a small fee.

A very spacious museum, its grand rooms are tastefully arranged with earthenware, maps, treasures from sunken galleons, furniture and paintings, an armory section and a

wonderful apothecary, set out like a cook's kitchen. Outside is a sundial, which enabled the judges seated in the court to tell the time.

✚ *Santo Domingo 6b* ✉ Calle Las Damas, Zona Colonial ☎ 682 4202 ⏰ Thu–Tue 9–5 💵 Moderate

### MUSEO DEL HOMBRE DOMINICANO

Although big and off-putting, the Museo del Hombre Dominicano (Museum of the Dominican Man) is actually just two floors of exhibitions, but definitely worth a visit. It begins with finds from archaeological digs that predate the Taino Indians, as far back as 3000 BC. An excellent collection of Taino objects hails from the north and east of the country. Most of the items were unearthed in a massive site near Boca Chica, and are important because of their variety and condition. To archaeologists the site is considered the jewel of the Antilles. A former director of the museum, Professor Dato Pagán Perdomo, was an authority on Indian rock art and has written many books on findings from his own expeditions. A glass cabinet contains skeletons of Tainos resting in the fetal position. Other highlights include stone images of Taino gods, the principal god was Tri gonolito, depicted with a triangular image, but you'll also see a crescent-shaped head which is the God of the Moon. Moving upwards, the museum deals with the actions of the Spanish conquistadors and the culture, Catholicism and cockfighting they introduced. Information boards are in Spanish, but an English and French guide is available.

✚ *Santo Domingo 1c* ✉ Plaza de la Cultura ☎ 687 3622 🕐 Tue–Sun 10–5 💰 Inexpensive

## MUSEO MUNDO DE AMBAR

Santo Domingo's Museo Mundo de Ambar (Amber Museum) has a tremendous collection of Dominican amber and examples of amber

from around the world. Pieces are for sale in the souvenir shop downstairs. Look for the fossilized butterfly in one fragment and an absolutely exquisite carved Taino god. Explanations are in English and there are also guided tours. At the back of the shop is an open workroom where craftsmen fashion beads from the amber. The rare larimar stone is also on display.

🚩 *Santo Domingo 5b* ✉ Calle Arzobispo Meriño 462, Zona Colonial ☎ 682 3309 🕓 Mon–Sat 9–6 ✋ Inexpensive

## MUSEO NACIONAL DE HISTORIA Y GEOGRÁFIA

In the newer part of Santo Domingo is Plaza de la Cultura, featuring the national theater fronted by a statue of Giuseppe Verdi. Nearby is a modern art gallery and a crop of museums. Museo Nacional de Historia y Geográfia (National History and Geography Museum) has a car, punctured with eight bullet holes. Its boot (trunk) is where the body of dictator Trujillo was bundled following his assassination in 1961. An assortment of objects connected with the Trujillo terror era, including his death mask and a replica of an electric chair are also on display – perhaps the most chilling being the copy of a photograph taken whilst one poor man was being electrocuted.

🚩 *Santo Domingo 1c* ✉ Plaza de la Cultura ☎ 686 6668 🕓 Tue–Sun 10–5 ✋ Inexpensive

## PALACIO NACIONAL

The Palacio Nacional (National Palace) was built from marble in 1947 on Trujillo's instructions, as a pale, mandarin-colored replica of the White House in Washington DC. Seat of the country's government, it is massive, bordered by wrought-iron railings, and is guarded by the military. It stands opposite the Ministry of Tourism in an area of the city known as Gazcue. You'll see many wealthy houses with intricate balconies, mainly because Trujillo drew in many important white immigrants, some of whom were architects. Nowadays those with money are tempted to the outskirts of the city, away from the traffic.

✚ *Santo Domingo 3c* ✉ Avenida México ☎ 695 8000 🕓 VIP tours by appointment ✋ Free

## PANTEÓN NACIONAL

The Panteón Nacional (National Pantheon) was originally a Jesuit church, built from 1714 to 1748. It was restored and renamed by Trujillo in 1958 to celebrate an international fair. Inside are the tombs of heroes of the independence struggle. Above and in front of the altar hangs a chandelier, a present from General Franco of Spain. Above the pews are what the guide tells you are iron screens bearing the swastika sign, a gift from Adolf Hitler of Germany. A flame for the heroes is forever lit at the foot of the altar. The best time to be here is at noon, when the national anthem is played and there's a changing of the guard.

✚ *Santo Domingo 6c* ✉ Calle de las Damas, Zona Colonial 🕓 Tue–Sun 8–6, Mon 2–6 ✋ Free

## PARQUE COLÓN

Parque Colón (Columbus Park) is a bustling square of shoe-shine boys, sidewalk sweepers and workers grabbing a quick coffee. It has a cigar shop with a mobile hut that offers prospective buyers a free smoke under the nearby fig tree. Loved by the pigeons, the bronze statue of Columbus, sculpted by Ernesto Gilbert, a French

sculptor, was inaugurated in 1887 as a present from France. Some say Columbus's left hand points north to La Isabela (➤ 48), the first settlement of the New World, others say to Asia, his intended destination. His right hand rests on a compass and a map. At each corner is a ship's masthead, symbolizing his four voyages to the Americas. Adjacent to the park are the Palacio de Borgellá (the presidential palace of the Haitian governors from 1822 to 1844), which now houses the tourism office, and the cathedral.

✚ *Santo Domingo 6c* ✉ Zona Colonial ❓ Cigar demonstrations Thu–Sun
ℹ 103 Calle Isabel la Católica ☎ 686 3858 ⏰ Mon–Fri 9–4

### RUINAS DEL HOSPITAL SAN NICOLÁS DE BARI

The ruins of the first hospital in the Americas, the Ruinas del Hospital San Nicolás de Bari have not succumbed to restoration. Built from 1503, the hospital survived the plunders of Sir Francis Drake. Today pigeons inhabit its crumbled arches, walled on one side by mahogany trees.

✚ *Santo Domingo 5c* ✉ Calle Hostos, Zona Colonial 🕐 Daily 👊 Free

### ZONA COLONIAL

Best places to see ➤ 54–55.

## HOTELS

### ▼▼▼Clarion Hotel Santo Domingo ($$)

Located in the center of the commercial and financial district of Santo Domingo, and near to the main shopping malls. More than 200 rooms, plus gym, restaurant and bars.

✉ Avenida Tiradentes, esquina Presidente Gonzales ☎ 541 6226; www.choicehotels.com

### ▼▼▼Courtyard by Marriott Santo Domingo ($$)

A beautiful location, right in the heart of the Zona Colonial, near historic monuments, palaces and the cathedral. Features an on-site courtyard café and restaurant and a swimming pool.

✉ Avenida Maximo Gomez ☎ 685 1010; www.marriot.com

### ▼▼ ▼▼ Hilton Santo Domingo ($$–$$$)

Set on the *malecón*, next door to an area of boutiques, restaurants and theaters, this fairly new hotel rising 21 storeys high has panoramic views of the Caribbean Sea. Features a health center with a range of treatments.

✉ 500 Avenida Washington ☎ 685 0000; www.hilton.com

### ▼▼Hotel Santo Domingo ($$–$$$)

Well situated within reach of the museums, Zona Colonial and shopping. Outdoor pool, sauna, three lit tennis courts and an exercise room. Massages available.

✉ Avenida Independencia esquina Abraham Lincoln ☎ 221 1511; www.hotelsantodomingo.com.do

### ▼▼▼Quality Hotel Santo Domingo ($$)

Full-service hotel located just five minutes from Las Americas International Airport and just 25 minutes from Santo Domingo. A choice of 120 plus guest rooms with views of the Caribbean Sea.

✉ Km 22 Autopista Las Americas ☎ 549 2525; www.choicehotels.com

### ▼▼▼Sofitel Frances Santo Domingo ($$–$$$)

See pages 78–79.

## RESTAURANTS

### ♦♦El Conuco ($$)

A rustic, country-style restaurant decorated with hammocks and locally woven textiles, and domino tables. A wholesome menu featuring steaks, chicken, stews and the Dominican specialties of white rice, beans, meat and fried plantains.

✉ Calle Casimiro de Moya ☎ 686 0129 🕐 Daily noon–2:30am

### ♦♦♦El Meson de la Cava ($$–$$$)

A stunning setting for this restaurant, built into a naturally formed cavern, 50ft (15m) below the surface. Visit for cocktails, then dinner and evening shows.

✉ Avenida Miradol Sur 1 ☎ 533 2818; www.mesondelacava.com
🕐 Daily noon–1am

### ♦♦Museo del Jamon ($)

Not a museum but a pub with aged shanks of ham curing and hanging from its beamed ceiling. Point to the one you want and it's pulled down and sliced. Other dishes include seafood, chicken and pork.

✉ Calle Atarazana 17 ☎ 688 9644 🕐 Daily 11am–late

### ♦♦Pat'e Palo Brasserie ($–$$)

See pages 58–59.

### ♦♦♦El Patio ($$–$$$)

See pages 58–59.

### ♦♦♦Reina de Espana ($$$)

A medieval-style villa that is often referred to as "the castle". A diverse blend of cuisine featuring local Dominican specialties, and also Spanish, Italian and French. Chose from seafood, beef, veal, goat and lamb.

✉ Cervantes/Santiago streets, near *malecón* ☎ 685 2588
🕐 Daily noon–midnight

### 🔻🔻🔻Restaurante Cantabrico ($$$)

A Spanish-style restaurant decorated with works by local artists, serving seafood, meats and good local Dominican favorites.

✉ Avenida Independencia ☎ 687 5101; www.restaurantcantabrico.com.do
🕐 Daily 11am–midnight

### 🔻🔻🔻Restaurant Don Pepe ($$)

An elegant and sophisticated restaurant with food prepared with Spanish flair. Menu features dishes with beef, chicken, pork and seafood and a well-praised choice of desserts.

✉ Pasteur Avenida/Santiago Esq ☎ 686 8481 🕐 Daily noon–4, 7–midnight

### 🔻🔻Samurai ($$)

See pages 58–59.

### 🔻🔻🔻Vesuvio ($$)

Facing the Caribbean Sea, this spectacularly-placed restaurant serves a medley of Dominican dishes and international specialties. Open since 1954, Vesuvio has built up a good reputation for sophisticated dining complemented by fine food and wines.

✉ 251 Avenida George Washington ☎ 221 1954 🕐 Daily noon–late

# SHOPPING

The focus of shopping is El Conde in Zona Colonial, a pedestrianized street, which is now a tourist street selling souvenirs, crafts and cigars. The more upmarket stores have good quality cigars, rum, ceramic faceless dolls, art, *merengue* CDs and wooden African carvings.

### Columbus Plaza

This gift shop mall in the Colonial Zone offers shops selling amber and larimar, a range of ethnic art plus a place to buy genuine Dominican cigars.

✉ Calle Arzobispo Meriño 105 ☎ 689 0565 🕐 Mon–Sat 9–7, Sun 9–noon

### Fabrica de Tabacos

A well-stocked tobacco shop where you can actually see cigars being hand-rolled. There is also a museum upstairs.

✉ Parque Colón, Zona Colonial, Santo Domingo ☎ 535 4448 ◷ Daily 9–6

## Juan Medina

One of many Dominican artists to have gallery space in the historic colonial zone, Juan Medina has worked on many government projects including the 150th anniversary of the Dominican Republic. He is also Director of the School of Fine Arts in the city.

✉ Calle Mercedes 153, Zona Colonial ☎ 221 4605 ◷ By appointment

## Mercado Modelo

Just north of the Zona Colonial, this market offers a full range of souvenirs. Quality is generally "mass-market" but there's some colorful fun stuff.

✉ Avenida Mella ☎ 686 6772 ◷ Daily 8–6

## Museo Mundo de Amber

Within the town's amber museum (▶ 95), the gift shop includes a fabulous collection of souvenirs and trinkets from inexpensive, quirky keyrings to pricey amber pieces set in silver and gold.

✉ Calle Arzobispo Meriño, Zona Colonial ☎ 682 3309 ◷ Mon–Sat 8:30–6, Sun 9–1

## Plaza Central

The country's biggest shopping center, with air-conditioned floors of banks, boutiques, furniture, ornaments, sportswear, jewelry, children's toys and clothing. Elevators and escalators rise above a fountain to the cinema, restaurants and nightclubs at the top.

✉ 27 de Febrero and Winston Churchill ☎ 567 5012 ◷ Daily (some parts on Sundays, plus entertainment)

# ENTERTAINMENT

El Boulevado, which has a sculpture park with a wrought-iron clock tower, is a lively, neon-lit thoroughfare at night. In Zona Colonial try Plaza de la Hispanidad. Along La Atarazana reputable restaurants serve delicious food and host regular flamenco and other music performances.

## NIGHTLIFE

### Bobo's

Currently one of the cool haunts for the capital's young crowd, this is a contemporary bar and restaurant that's a great place for people watching while you enjoy a cocktail or two.

✉ Calle Hostos ☎ 689 1183 ⏱ Mon–Sat noon–3, 6–1

### Guácara Taina

Situated in a huge bat cave. Live *merengue* and salsa makes it very busy on weekends.

✉ Mirador Sur ☎ 533 1051 ⏱ Nightly (closed Mon)

### Hard Rock Café

The well-established combination of American fast food and music brings its recipe to downtown Santo Domingo.

✉ Calle El Conde 103, Zona Colonial, Santo Domingo ☎ 686 7771
⏱ Sun–Thu 11:30am–12:30am, Fri–Sat 11:30am-1:30am

### Jet Set

*Merengue* music. Every Monday and Thursday a visiting *merengue* orchestra plays (entry fee).

✉ Avenida Indepencia No 2253 ☎ 533 9707 ⏱ Nightly

### Jubilee

The smartest clubs in town for a while now, Friday and Saturday sees a stream of trendy "movers and shakers" networking and having fun. Worth getting dressed up for.

✉ Renaissance Jaragua Hotel, Avenida George Washington 367
☎ 221 2222 ⏱ Tue–Sat 9–4

### Trio Cafe

High-class bar with an often wealthy clientele.

✉ Lincoln Avenida ☎ 412 0964 ⏱ Nightly

## CASINOS

The capital has several casinos where you can try your luck at the tables or the slot machines. You'll generally find them housed within the major hotels. Dress smart casual (no shorts and T-shirts) and carry your passport or identity card.

### Renaissance Jaragua Hotel and Casino

✉ Avenida George Washington 367 ☎ 221 2222; www.marriott.com

### Hotel Santo Domingo

✉ Avenida Independencia esquina Abraham Lincoln ☎ 221 1511; www.hotelsantodomingo.com.do

### Hotel El Napolitano

✉ Avenida George Washington 101 ☎ 689 5579

## THEATER

### Casa de Teatro

Comprehensive program of plays, ballet and theater here.

✉ Arzobispo Meriño 14, Santo Domingo ☎ 689 3430

### Teatro Nacional

Modern building hosting opera, ballet and orchestral concerts.

✉ Plaza de la Cultura, Santo Domingo ☎ 687 3191 ❓ Smart dress only

## SPORTS

### Baseball (Beisol)

The season runs from October to January. The main venues are in Santo Domingo and San Pedro de Macoris.

✉ Santo Domingo ☎ Ligue de Baseball 567 3671 or National Stadium for Baseball 540 5772

### The Olympic Park (Sports Palace)

Used for the 2003 Pan American Olympic Games. The park caters for basketball and softball, and has an aquatics center, velodrome, and volleyball pavillion.

✉ Avenida Ortega y Gasset/Avenida 27 de Febrero, Santo Domingo

# The North

Puerto
Plata

Santiago de los
Caballeros

**In addition to
its exquisite beaches
and deep green national
parks, the north has
amber. The Dominican
Republic is famous for the
variety and clarity of its amber and its astounding
collection of fossils and jewelry.**

Found in the mountains between Puerto Plata and Santiago,
amber is mined by hand, using picks and shovels. It is the
fossilized sap from a type of carob tree that existed millions of
years ago. Prized pieces contain fossilized insects and plants that
became caught and embedded in the sticky, honey-like substance
before it hardened. Also not found anywhere else in the world is
larimar, a powder-blue stone believed to be either a variety of
pectolite or a fossil. The biggest larimar mines are midway
between Barahona and Baoruco in the southwest.

### BAHÍA DE SAMANÁ
Best places to see ➤ 38–39.

### CABARETE
If you don't rise early enough to grab a sun
lounger at lively Cabarete, then you could
perch at a beach bar drinking cold Presidente beer to *merengue*
tunes. This favorite holiday haunt is a windsurfing and kiteboarding
center – boards line up like dominoes on the beach. This is a good
place to rent equipment and organize eco-tours, mountain bicycle
trips, and adventure safaris into the country's interior from the
throng of adventure tour operators. Shop here, too, for sarongs,
jewelry, and Taino-style art. People read newspapers and have
breakfast at French or German bakeries serving Belgian waffles.
Seafood restaurants and bars spill onto the beach. At night, happy
hours and free spaghetti evenings take over. If you tire of
Cabarete, then flit to nearby Sosúa and back in a *gua-gua*.

✚ 7B 🚌 *Gua-gua* from Puerto Plata and Sosúa
ℹ 571 0962

### FUERTE DE SAN FELIPE
The rounded walls of Fuerte de San Felipe
(San Felipe Fort) once protected the Bahía
de Puerto Plata, the port you can see in
the background. Built by the Spaniards and
completed in the 16th century, the fort
was supposed to deter invasions from
French buccaneers and other pirates, yet
was never used in battle. Until the end of
the Trujillo era in the 1960s, the fort served
as a prison. Duarte, hero of independence,
may have been held here. Deep within the
fort's chambers is a scant collection of
cannon and musket balls, and black-leaded

fragments of 16th-century artillery. From its turrets you face the Atlantic, like the rusty cannons. A coral-bottomed moat, now empty, once had lethal spikes hidden beneath the water.

✚ 6B ✉ Avenida Gregorio Luperón ☎ 586 2318 🕓 Tue–Sun 11–5

## ISLA DE CAYO LEVANTADO

This spectacular island covered with tropical forest and with a trio of excellent beaches is supposedly where several glamorous Bacardi adverts were filmed. The island bay has recently seen the opening of one of the Dominican Republic's latest five-star all inclusive resorts (Bahia Principe), but for those not resident, day trips stop off – usually after whale watching – to enjoy a spot of swimming and relaxation. The main beach, bedecked with dining tables and shacks selling coco-loco and kitsch souvenirs, is often packed with tour groups having buffet lunches.

✚ 12D 🍴 If not on a tour, take a picnic ❌ Arroya Barril, Samaná
❓ Can be visited on a whale-watching tour (► 124) or by water taxi from Samaná dock

### LAGUNA GRI-GRI

Laguna Gri-Gri (Gri-Gri Lagoon), a popular day trip, usually involves a bus ride to Río San Juan fishing village and then a two-hour boat ride through the mangroves and out onto the ocean. Charter your own boat if you wish. Look for strange rock formations, caves of stalactites, stalagmites, and swallow birds. Remember to take insect spray and a towel because there's a refreshing swimming spot.

⊞ 8B ⊠ San Juan ⊛ Daily ✋ Inexpensive ⊟ Express bus to San Juan from Santo Domingo then *gua-gua*

### MONUMENTO A LOS HÉROES, SANTIAGO

Best places to see ➤ 46–47.

### MUSEO DE AMBAR DOMINICANO

The Museo de Ambar Dominicano (Dominican Amber Museum) in Puerto Plata is one of the best places to see amber. Occupying a brilliant-white, 19th-century building that was a hotel then a school, the museum is marked by its own version of the Jurassic Park movie logo. The second floor of the museum boasts a scorpion, a praying mantis, petals and leaves fossilized in chunks of amber. The priceless trapped lizard has been dated at 50 million years old. The museum's English-speaking guide whisks you around the objects, and demonstrates how to distinguish fake, plastic "amber" jewelry from the real thing by dropping each into water. Larimar is particularly exquisite when set in silver – the museum has a stunning collection.

**www**.ambermuseum.com

✚ 6B ✉ Calle Duarte 61, Puerto Plata ☎ 586 2848 🕔 Mon–Sat 9–6 ✋ Inexpensive 🚌 Luperón, Puerto Plata

## PARQUE HISTORICO LA ISABELA

Best places to see ➤ 48–49.

## PARQUE LUPERÓN

The heart of Puerto Plata (➤ 52) is Parque Luperón (Luperón Park), commonly known as Parque Central. Its pretty Glorieta Sicilian pavilion was built in 1872. Nineteenth-century buildings, including the town hall and law courts, surround the park. The art deco Catedral de San Felipe is worth a peek inside. From here thread streets of cafés, more gingerbread-style houses, the Museo

de Ambar Dominicano (➤ 109) boutiques and souvenir shops.

🚹 6B 🖂 Puerto Plata 🖐 Free ✖ Gral G. Luperón, Puerto Plata

## PARQUE NACIONAL LOS HAÏTISES

To the south of the Bahía de Samaná, Parque Nacional Los Haïtises (National Park Los Haïtises) is a microcosm of limestone hillocks covered with tropical humid forest, bamboo, swamp and coral knolls that jut out into the ocean.

Birds thrive here, particularly the elusive Hispaniolan parakeet, herons and American frigates. Other attractions are the Taino caves decorated with drawings and rock carvings. Cueva de Angel, a cave with birds and tropical forest, is a frequent tourist stop. Remote and rugged, the park is best visited on an organized tour.

🚹 10E

ℹ National parks office ☎ 472 3717

# a drive along the Amber Coast

Although amber is mined further inland, the coastal strip from east to west is nicknamed the Amber Coast. Driving westwards, expect to meet cattle being driven by boys on horseback and chickens crossing the road. Children straddle donkeys carrying pails of water and vegetables.

*From Cabarete head along Carretera 5, through palms and mahogany trees, passing airport signs and big resorts until you reach Sosúa.*

To see Sosúa beach, park on the right, just before the village (look for the black and white Harrison sign) and walk down the stone steps.

*Continue on the same road toward Puerto Plata and either explore the town or make your way to Luperón (first following signs to Santiago before you spot the detour to Luperón).*

The route is through crops of coffee, avocados, corn and bananas. Sugarcane fields are dotted with royal palms. Notice the average house is a simple bohío, similar to the wooden-slatted shacks occupied by the Taino Indians. Despite their primitive appearance, the bohíos are well-kept and painted in striking pinks, greens and blues.

*From here the way is signposted to Parque Historico La Isabela (➤ 48). Once you've explored the park, continue past the church.*

In 1992, Mass was said by Pope John Paul II to commemorate Columbus's discovery.

*You can either retrace your journey back to Cabarete or head for a longer stay at Puerto Plata and the Museo de Ambar Dominicano (Dominican Amber Museum, ➤ 109).*

**Distance** 109 miles (176km) maximum
**Time** Full day
**Start point** Cabarete ✚ 7B
**End point** Parque Historico La Isabela ✚ 4A
**Lunch** Numerous in Puerto Plata or Rancho del Sol, Parque Historica La Isabela ($–$$)

### PARQUE NACIONAL MONTE CRISTI

The Parque Nacional Monte Cristi (National Park Monte Cristi) gives you a feeling of being in the Australian outback, although pure white sands, aqua-blue oceans and mangroves remind you it's the Caribbean. A motor boat takes you across the coastal swamp to a wooden lookout tower to spot manatees. To date it's mainly Dominicans who swim from the beautiful beach and picnic here on Sundays, though it has obvious potential for development as an adventure destination. There are plans to create a paved road. For now either take a 4x4 vehicle along the bumpy access road or book a tour to the Haitian border that includes Parque Nacional La Isabela and Monte Cristi.

✚ 2B ✉ Caño Estero Hondo, Bay of La Isabela ⏰ Daily 8–5 🍴 Take a picnic 👋 Inexpensive ❓ Use mosquito repellent, and wear a sun hat ℹ National park office ☎ 472 3717

### PICO ISABEL DE TORRES

Named by Columbus after the Queen of Spain, Pico Isabel de Torres is the unmistakable, 2,624ft (800m) peak, thickly clad with green vegetation, that towers over Puerto Plata. On its slopes is a scientific reserve while the top has a botanical garden, magnificent views and Cristo Redentor, a statue of Christ. Depending on whether the Caribbean's first electric cable car, the volatile *teléferico*, is working, you might be able to ride for 13 minutes to the summit. For now you can drive to it (4x4 recommended) or hike, or mountain-bicycle down from the peak.

✚ 6B ☎ 586 2122 🕙 Cable car: daily 8:30–5 (times may vary)
✋ Inexpensive ❓ Tours with Iguana Mama ➤ 124

## PLAYA DORADA

Playa Dorada is the biggest resort complex in the Caribbean, sprawling over 247 acres (100ha) and edged by a 2-mile (3km), caramel-colored curve of sand. Guests at its 14 all-inclusive hotels are identified by different-colored plastic bracelets. Despite its 4,500-plus rooms, between February and March you'd be hard-pressed to find a bed – reservations are highly recommended. The 18-hole Robert Trent Jones golf course (which boasts 10 tees overlooking the Atlantic Ocean) and a shopping plaza within the complex supplement each hotel's own restaurants, nightclubs and casinos. Non-residents can sometimes buy a day pass. Walk the beach, ride the banana boat, rest under a palm umbrella or snorkel off the stone jetties. Toward the western stretch of the beach, low tide exposes a patchwork of seaweed-strewn rock pools where children gather to watch the fish.

✚ 6B ✉ Puerto Plata
☎ 291 0001 ✈ Gral G. Luperón, Puerto Plata

## PLAYA GRANDE

Over half a mile (1km) long with high cliffs and shaded by palm trees, Playa Grande is one of the finest beaches in the country. This upscale area is very popular with golfers.

✚ 9B

## PUERTO PLATA

Best places to see ➤ 52–53.

## SANTIAGO DE LOS CABALLEROS

At the heart of the country's tobacco industry and set within the fertile Valle Cibao (Cibao Valley) is Santiago de los Caballeros, the country's second largest city. Known simply as Santiago, the place buzzes day and night – what *merengue* is not played on street corners is blasted from passing cars that are patched and home-painted.

Present-day Santiago sprawls on the banks of the Río Yaque del Norte. (The city founded by Bartolomé

Columbus in 1495 at another site was largely destroyed by the 1562 earthquake.) Aside from the Monumento a los Héroes de la Restauración de la República (Heroes Monument, ➤ 46), Santiago has a handful of attractions. Although not as pretty as Puerto Plata's main square, Parque Duarte (Duarte Park) has the ubiquitous shoeshine boys and *merengue* cassette music sellers. The Museo del Tabaco (Tobacco Museum) traces the history of the uses of tobacco from the 16th century. Provided you are smartly dressed, you can glimpse inside the grand, members-only Centro de Recreo club, built in 1894. Next door is a Palacio Consistorial gallery, the former town hall, and quite empty apart from whatever temporary exhibitions it is hosting at the time, maybe carnival masks, sculpture or paintings. The 19th-century Catedral Santiago Apòstol, as pink as a birthday cake, has an interior of mahogany, brightly colored stained glass and gold leaf.

If you just want to shop, Santiago has roughly made, inexpensive and cheerful clothing, watches, wallets, shoes, carnival masks and fast food. A new vibrant center, the Centro Cultural Eduardo León Jimenes, located in the town showcases works by local artists (Avenida 27 de Febrero 146; open Tue–Sun 10–7).

➕ 6C 🚌 Express bus from Santo Domingo and Puerto Plata
❓ English-speaking guides offer tours ✖ Cibao, Santiago

## SOSÚA

Away from the busy main highway, Sosúa consists of leafy lanes of bars, boutiques and restaurants serving Italian, Mexican and – more unusually – much German fare. In 1940 many Jewish refugees from Nazi Europe settled here. It has been suggested that dictator Trujillo was keen to earn international respect, or that he wanted to "whiten" his country after years of black Haitian immigration. Anyway, Trujillo set aside a portion of land for the Jewish immigrants to work. The Jews, however, were not farmers but intellectuals and businessmen. Still, they brought their tastes with them and made Sosúa famous for its butter, cheese and sausages. Few Jewish houses remain, though the synagogue can be visited. At one end of town is a mixture of tin roof shacks, at the other the half-moon curve of the popular El Batey bay, a highlight of the north. Reached via a stone flight of stairs, the beach is beyond the network of paintings, cigars, beachwear and even a barber and his chair, ready to cut. Swimming is very safe here – the bay is protected by a coral reef – which is a reason why so many fish are spotted by snorkelers and passengers of glass-bottomed boats. There's a jazz festival every October at venues in both Sosúa and nearby Cabarete where a sandcastle-building competition is also held during February.

🕂 7B 🚌 *Gua-gua* from Puerto Plata ✈ Gral G. Luperón, Puerto Plata ❓ English-speaking guides offer tours

ℹ Edificio Gel Brown 2a, Autopista Luperón
☎ 571 3433

## LAS TERRENAS

Although Las Terrenas, originally a fishing village, has been taken over by around a dozen Italian, French and German hotels and a string of restaurants, it is loved by many visitors to the Dominican Republic who shy away from the sprawling all-inclusive resorts. The beaches of El Portillo and quieter Playa Bonita are favorites, offering scuba diving and other water sports. The nearby village of El Limón gives access to the Salto de Caloda, an impressive, high waterfall.

🕂 10D 🚌 *Gua-gua* or pick-up truck ✈ Arroya Barril, Samaná

# HOTELS

### ♦♦Caribe Switzinn ($$)

With only four guest rooms, the Caribe Switzinn feels like a private villa. The whitewashed Spanish style villa is set in tropical gardens and there's a restaurant and pool on site. It is located 3.7 miles (6km) from the sea but has regular transfers and can arrange water sports equipment rental and excursions.

✉ Off highway 5, Payita, La Entrada ☎ 633 2366; www.caribeswitzinn.com

### ♦♦♦Club Hotel Riu Bachata ($$–$$$)

Located on the beach in Maimon Bay and surrounded by tropical gardens. Within the complex of the Club Hotels Riu Bachata and Riu Mambo. You can use the main building facilities at the Mambo and all-inclusive water sports and introductory scuba diving.

✉ Bahia de Mamon, Puerta Plata ☎ 320 1010; www.riu.com

### ♦♦♦Club Hotel Riu Mambo ($–$$)

Bright and bustling all-inclusive hotel set on a beach, with a full range of activities and evening entertainment. Restaurants, lounge bars, beach bar cafés, two swimming pools, children's pool and Caribbean Street with spa, hairdressers and stores.

✉ Bahia de Mamon, Puerta Plata ☎ 320 1212; www.riu.com

### ♦♦♦Club Hotel Riu Merengue ($$)

Set on the beach, in Maimon Bay, with the Club Hotels Riu Bachata and Mambo. Once again there is use of the main building facilities (see above).

✉ Bahia de Mamon, Puerta Plata ☎ 320 4000; www.riu.com

### Hotel Gran Bahia Principe Cayacoa ($$$)

See pages 78–79.

### ♦♦Hotel Todo Blanco ($–$$)

See pages 78–79.

### ♦♦La Palmas Residence ($$)

See pages 78–79.

### ▼▼▼ Oasis Marien Hotel ($–$$)

A new all-inclusive property, with a relaxing spa and evening entertainment.

✉ Carretera Luperon, Puerta Plata ☎ 320 1515; www.globalia-hotels.com

### ▼▼▼ Occidental Grand Flamenco Puerta Plata ($$–$$$)

Just 15 minutes from the airport on Playa Dorada beach, and surrounded by the 18-hole golf course designed by Robert Trent Jones. Also located ten minutes from Puerta Plata town.

✉ Playa Dorada Beach, Puerta Plata ☎ 320 5084;
www.occidentalhotels.com

### ▼▼▼ Viva Wyndham Tangerine ($$$)

Set in verdant forest just three minutes by taxi from central Cabarete, the all-inclusive Viva Wyndham offers over 300ft (91m) of beachfront. The hotel provides a good range of land and water sports provision including mountain biking, riding, rafting, diving and kite-surfing, or try the salsa and *merengue* lessons that will set you up for a night at the disco.

✉ Carretera Sosua-Cabarete, Cabarete ☎ 571 0381; www.wyndham.com

## RESTAURANTS

### Brasserie Barrio Latino ($–$$)

An open-air French restaurant with a huge menu and varied from breakfast to snacks to dinner, plus good value daily specials.

✉ El Paseo, Las Terrenas ☎ 240 6367 🕐 Mon–Sat 7:30–midnight

### Café Cito ($)

This funky Canadian-run eatery acts as a kind of meeting place and info exchange for the English speakers in the area. Enjoy good continental cuisine and regular live music.

✉ Plaza Isabela, Km 3.5 Puerto Plata-Sosua highway, Puerto Plata
☎ 586 7923; www.cafecito.info 🕐 Mon–Sat 11–midnight, Sun 5–midnight

### La Casa del Pescador ($)

Right on the beach, in the heart of Cabarete town, this is, of course, a great restaurant for seafood and the daily catch. From fish consommé and seafood salads to freshly caught lobster, grilled octopus and shrimp. Also serving pastas, meats and surf 'n' turf specials. Great setting.

✉ Cabarete ☎ 571 0760; www.lacasadelpescador.com

🕔 Daily 10am–11pm

## Chino ($$)

Chinese food is a rare find in the Dominican Republic. Chino also serves good local dishes too. There's a great terrace with panoramic views across the Bahia de Samana.

✉ Calle Santa Bárbara, Santa Bárbara de Samana ☎ 538 2215

🕔 Daily 11–11

## Hemingway's Café ($)

See pages 58–59.

## Morua Mai ($–$$$)

Established by German owners in the 1970s, this restaurant has the feel of a European café with tables and chairs on the sidewalk. A selection of local seafood specialties, steaks and chicken dishes are all accompanied by a good selection of wines or local beer.

✉ Pedro Clisante 5, El Batay, Sosua ☎ 571 2966 🕔 Daily 8am–midnight

## On the Waterfront ($$–$$$)

This longstanding restaurant is still as popular as ever for its delicious seafood – and the waterfront location of course.

✉ The Waterfront Hotel, Calle Dr Rosen, Sosúa ☎ 571 2670

🕔 Daily 7am–11pm

## Pescador ($$–$$)

On the main street in Las Galeras, this recently refurbished Spanish owned restaurant concentrates on seafood dishes. There's a nice outdoor patio for al fresco dining.

✉ Calle Las Galeras, Las Galeras ☎ 538 0052 🕔 Daily 8–11:30

## La Salsa ($$)

This refurbished fishing shack is known for its Dominican dishes "like mama used to make" and its excellent fresh seafood. The extensive drinks list also make it a great place for evening aperitifs.

✉ Calle Playa Cacao, Las Terrenas ☎ 260 6805 ◷ Daily noon–midnight

### Sam's Bar ($–$$)

A great ex-pat meeting place when nothing but American-style fast food will do, Sam's Bar does a great line in full cooked breakfast and piping hot coffee.

✉ Calle José del Carmen Ariza 37, Puerto Plata ☎ 586 2767
◷ Daily 7am–midnight

## SHOPPING

### Haitian Caraibes Art Gallery

Las Terrenas has more than a handful if art galleries but this is considered one of the best for its range of original Dominican and Haitian paintings. Prices can rise steeply for certain artists, but what better way to start, or add to, your collection.

✉ Avenida Duarte 159, Las Terrenas ☎ 240 6250 ◷ Mon–Sat 9–1, 4–8

### Harrisons

A reputable jeweler with branches around the island and in several hotels. Fine jewelry of amber and larimar, and Dominican black jade – "Jadite," a hard stone but soft in appearance.

✉ Plaza Isabela, Puerta Plata ☎ 586 3933 ◷ Daily 8–6

### Playa Dorada Plaza

Part of the massive Playa Dorada complex of resorts on the north coast. A bright and busy place with a range of stores selling souvenirs, fashion, music and personal necessities.

✉ Playa Dorada ☎ 320 2000 ◷ Daily 9am–9pm

### Plaza Turisol

The largest mall on the north coast with over 80 different shops offers a range of souvenirs from tropical clothing to art and crafts, including another outlet of Domenico Premium Cigar Factory.

✉ Avenida Luperon, Puerto Plata ◷ Daily 9–9

## ENTERTAINMENT

### Bambu

Perennial nightspot that's on everyone's list of must-visit venues when in the Cabarete area. Drop in for an early evening drink and you might not leave until the early hours. Great celebrity DJs.

✉ On the waterfront, Main Street, Cabarete ☎ 982 4549; www.bambucabarete.com 🕐 Daily 9am–4am

### Lax

This cool bar/nightclub is one of the most popular places in laid-back Cabarete Beach. There's a menu of light foods and snacks. Live music some evenings.

✉ Cabarete Beach ☎ 710 0569; www.lax-cabarete.com 🕐 Daily 11am–2am

### Voodoo Lounge

Classy spot in front of the Sosua Bay Hotel. Range of music plus karoke some nights.

✉ Sosua ☎ 571 3559

## SPORTS AND ACTIVITIES

### Iguana Mama

This long-established and well-recognized company offers a good range of tours and "adrenalin" sports including canyoning and cascading – not for the faint hearted!

✉ Calle Principal 74, Cabarete ☎ 571 0908; www.iguanamama.com

### Turinter

Offers a full range of adventure trips including jeep, truck and buggy safaris.

✉ Avenida Luis A Ginebra 24, Puerto Plata ☎ 586 3911; www.turinter.com

### Victoria Marine

Kim Beddall is a qualified scientist who runs fascinating whale-watching trips in Bahia de Samana (Samana Bay) daily in season (January to mid-March).

✉ Port, Santa Barbára de Samana ☎ 538 2494

# The Southeast

**Heading east from Santo Domingo on the Las Américas Highway and the motorway Autovía del Este (that begins just beyond the Las Américas airport), the landscape pales to dry, flat savannas. No coffee, tobacco or cocoa grows here, only scrub and sugarcane. At a railroad crossing with flashing red lights you may be delayed for a good ten minutes by a long train, laden with sugarcane stalks, bound for the sugar mill at La Romana. Inland you could make your own pilgrimage to the famous basilica at Higüey.**

San Pedro de Macorís

By the roadside you might see displays of freshly caught river crabs for sale. The region's exquisite beaches offer scores of opportunities for serious relaxation. At the far southeastern tip of the country is beautiful Parque Nacional del Este and the popular Isla Saona. You can travel back in time to the cliff-top village of Altos de Chavón (actually 20th-century but designed to look medieval) or go snorkeling on the coral reefs of Parque Nacional Submarino La Caleta.

### ALTOS DE CHAVÓN

Best place to see ➤ 36–37.

### BASÍLICA DE NUESTRA SEÑORA DE LA ALTAGRACIA

Higüey itself is a busy town with little to offer the tourist at first glance. It is, however, the country's most important religious site. Said to be built on the site where the Virgin Mary appeared in 1691, the Basílica de Nuestra Señora de la Altagracia is an extraordinary vision. The French architects André Jacques Dunoyer de Segonzac and Pierre Dupré have shaped its spire into a pair of hands praying. Started in 1952, the cathedral is made from solid concrete in such a way as to withstand a hurricane. Many children beg outside the basilica or sell you candles. Pilgrimages occur on January 21 and August 16. Pilgrims enter the shrine to La Altagracia (the Virgin of the Highest Grace), and touch a case displaying a 16th-century painting of the Virgin and a gold crown given as a gift by a former pope.

✚ 22J ⊠ Higüey ⊘ Daily 🚌 Bus from Santo Domingo
🛈 Calle Altagracia ☎ 554 2672

### BÁVARO

Bávaro, on the Costa del Coco (Coconut Coast), is paradise: blue skies, a blue sea and uninterrupted white sands sloping to calm, reef-protected waters. Some of the country's most exclusive resorts lie behind its palm-fringed beach. Tourists go sea fishing for marlin, while others merely tuck into freshly caught lobsters and langoustines grilled out in the open at restaurants scattered across the sands. Musical trios strum guitars and play *merengue* or sing romantic ballads. In short, it's the stuff of dream holidays.

✚ 24H ⊠ Costa del Coco 🚌 Bus to Higüey, then *gua-gua* ✖ Punta Aguila, Romana

# TESCO

ELGIN LOSSIE GREEN
any questions please visit
www.tesco.com/store-locator

DOG TREATS        *              £2.50

TOTAL                           £2.50
MASTERCARD SALE                 £2.50
  AID       : A0000000041010
  NUMBER    : ***********4197    ICC
  PAN SEQ NO : 00
  AUTH CODE : 030208
  MERCHANT  : 1800631
CHANGE DUE                      £0.00
*****************************************

## JOIN CLUBCARD TODAY
This visit could have earned you
2 Clubcard points.
To join, visit Tesco.com/clubcard/join ,
text 'Join' to 30850 or call us on
either 0800 591688 or 0800 591688

7/03/20  18:51  2489  076  9076  0525

Tesco Stores Ltd
Tesco House
Shire Park, Kestrel Way
Welwyn Garden City
Hertfordshire
AL7 1GA
**www.tesco.com**

VAT NO: 220430231

Thank you for shopping with us.

# TESCO
*Every little helps*

Should you change your mind about your
purchase, please return the product with your
proof of purchase, within 30 days, and we'll
happily offer a refund or replacement.

Conditions apply to some products.
Please see instore for details or
visit www.tesco.com/returns.

Tesco Stores Ltd
Tesco House
Shire Park, Kestrel Way
Welwyn Garden City
Hertfordshire
AL7 1GA
**www.tesco.com**

VAT NO: 220430231

Thank you for shopping with us.

# TESCO
*Every little helps*

Should you change your mind about your
purchase, please return the product with your

## BAYAHIBÈ

Bayahibè is another idyllic haunt and absolutely gorgeous, a gateway to Parque Nacional del Este (➤ 129). A colorful and hectic fishing village, Bayahibe is engulfed by pale-honey sands shaped as small coves, rolling down to azure lapping waters. La Laguna Beach has been awarded the European Blue Flag for high environmental management and safety standards. Waiting speedboats, catamarans and wooden craft ferry scores of people out to Isla Saona (➤ 42). If you haven't already organized a tour, it can prove expensive. Best to share a fishing boat called a *lancha* that works like a taxi – the more passengers, the cheaper the fare – or there's an excellent diving center.

✛ 22K

## CASA DE CAMPO

The resort of Casa de Campo at La Romana is today as big as a town, and has been dubbed "the Caribbean's most complete resort" now with a marina and yacht club and Portofino, a shopping and dining area. La Romana had been the country's primary sugar production center, but sugar production was taken over by industrial free trade zones, tobacco and the then-new "industry" of tourism. The mega-rich sugar plantation

owners anticipated these changes and diversified by building or buying hotels and resorts. In the 1960s the US company, Gulf &

Western, bought the sugar mill and invested heavily in La Romana. To entertain their visitors and top executives they transformed the Hotel La Romana into today's exclusive resort (although it's no longer owned by Gulf & Western). Casa de Campo suffered badly during Hurricane Georges in 1998 and has since been spectacularly rebuilt to the tune of US$24 million. It boasts championship-rated 18-hole golf courses, designed by Pete Dye, polo, clay pigeon shooting and all kinds of water sports.

**www.**casadecampo.com

➕ 22K ✉ La Romana ☎ 523 3333; ❌ Punta Aguila, Romana

### ISLA SAONA

Best place to see ➤ 42–43.

### PARQUE NACIONAL DEL ESTE

The fabulous Parque Nacional del Este (National Park of the East) is a ribbon of jade green sandwiched between a blue sky and a blue-green ocean. Here are breathtaking beauty, wildlife and solitude – its only human inhabitants live on Isla Saona (➤ 42) but keep an eye out for iguanas, and, offshore, dolphins and turtles. The park's limestone terraces are clothed with a mixture of subtropical humid, dry and deciduous forests. Its many limestone caves – José Maria Cave especially – are decorated with pre-Columbian petroglyphs and pictographs. Best access is by boat, perhaps as part of a day trip to Isla Saona. This can be organized in your resort or in Bayahibe (➤ 127).

➕ 22K 🕐 Daily 8–6 ❓ Boat trips arranged through operators

ℹ National parks office ☎ 472 3717

# a boat trip to Isla Saona

Either arrange a tour through your hotel or resort, or arrive at Bayahibe beach and reserve a transfer. More sightseeing can be had if you rent a fishing boat from the steps of Altos de Chavón (▶ 36).

The Mediterranean village of Altos de Chavón perches on the cliff tops as you chug through a corridor of palms, passing other people in boats, fishing. Boca de Chavón fishing village approaches as you turn left at the river mouth, into the expanse of Caribbean Sea. Heading east along this coastline you can see the extent of the all-inclusives. Guests perform aerobics on the beach, or paddle in kayaks, or try desperately to stay on windsurfers.

Suddenly the resorts thin out and disappear as you enter Parque Nacional del Este (▶ 129). Only forests, palm trees and sand line the shore. A boy riding his horse bareback might appear.

The water here is calm and clear. On the way your boat stops at a natural swimming

pool where starfish rest on the seabed a few yards (meters) below. You can take a dip or enjoy a drink from the boat's onboard icebox.

The boat continues through a lagoon lined with black and red mangroves between the mainland and Isla Saona. Finally arriving at the island, you head first to look at paintings and souvenirs in the fishing village. A two-minute journey then whisks you to the main beach, Punta Catuano, to relax for some hours until the boat returns the same way.

**Distance** 19 miles (30km)
**Time** Full day
**Start/end point** Altos de Chavón or Bayahibè ✚ 22J or 22K
❓ Reserve through your resort or rent a boat from Bayahibe
**Lunch** Usually provided by the tour and taken on the island. Otherwise buy provisions at the French bakery at Altos de Chavón or take a picnic. Don't forget drinking water, sunscreen and a camera, and hiking boots if going to the caves.

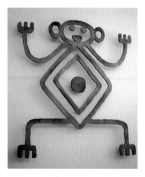

## PARQUE NACIONAL LA CALETA

From Santo Domingo the coastal road runs through groves of almond trees and palms. Roadside vendors sell carved pieces of calcium from the caves, etched bookends and other Taino-style souvenirs. You'll reach Parque Nacional La Caleta (La Caleta National Park), the smallest in the country. Between coral cliffs, its sandy cove has upturned fishing boats. You can swim and snorkel from here in shallow water, around a number of coral reefs sporting tropical fish and octopuses. Divers and underwater photographers especially find the sunken 20th-century wreck, the *Hickory*, of interest. Some of

the best deep water wrecks can be found in this part of the island. A one-storey building near the entrance is actually a museum sheltering a remarkable Indian cemetery (🕐 Mon–Fri 9–6), found in 1972 and excavated. The Indians buried their dead near the sea, in easily dug sand.

The haunting collection of skeletons, buried in the fetal position to await reincarnation, is at times grotesque, for when a chief died it was customary to bury his wife, alive, with him.

➕ 18J 🕐 Daily 8–6 👋 Inexpensive 🚌 *Gua-gua* from Santo Domingo
ℹ️ National parks office ☎ 472 3717

## PUNTA CANA

Best places to see ➤ 50–51.

### PLAYA BOCA CHICA

"Boca chica" means "little mouth" and Playa Boca Chica's beach is shaped like a bay. Said to be the Caribbean's largest natural swimming pool, the mirror-like stretch of water has no

crashing surf and is an effortless place to swim. The beach is popular with Santo Domingans who splash about with the tourists. Families with children wade out to a small island and, aside from swimming, go yachting, snorkeling, scuba diving or riding the banana boat. At the main entrance to the beach are wooden shacks selling fried fish and pizza-size rounds of batter called *yani queque*.

🚌 19J 🚍 Express bus from Parque Central, Santo Domingo or *gua-gua*

🛈 Calle Duarte esquina Caracol ☎ 523 5106

**133**

## SAN PEDRO DE MACORÍS

San Pedro de Macorís is a big, busy, and – thanks to the American occupation – a baseball-crazy town. It lies on the Río Higuamo, where the Americans landed in seaplanes. Good sugarcane yields in the early 20th century made the town rich, reflected in its grand Victorian architecture. Only a few beauties exist, including the English Gothic, brilliant-white Iglesia San Pedro. A more contemporary building, which takes center stage in the town, is a green-topped baseball stadium. The home team is the Estrellas Orientales and the locals are crazy about the sport. San Pedro de Macorís is home to some of the best baseball players in the world, including Sammy Sosa who was born here. They say

chewing the sweet fibers off bark-like sticks of sugarcane made the budding young players strong. This is also the base for exploring Cueva de las Maravillas, a cave of rock paintings from the Taino period. The opening of the cave is controversial, especially since the installation of lights and elevators.

➕ 20J ☎ Calle Ramòn Montalvo 10 ☎ 529 3644
🚌 *Gua-gua* from Santo Domingo

## HOTELS

### Barceló Premium Punta Cana ($$–$$$)

Set on Arena Gorda Beach, and attracting families, couples and singles. Facilities include a beach, tropical gardens, free-form pool, fine-dining restaurants and nightly entertainment. Sailing, surfing, snorkeling and diving also available.

✉ Playa Arena Gorda, Bávaro ☎ 476 7777; www.barcelo.com

### Casa de Campo Resort ($$$)

Internationally famous and dubbed "the Caribbean's most complete resort" – it's like a small town that you travel through on personal golf carts. Restaurants, shops and beautiful beach. Three 18-hole golf courses designed by Pete Dye including "The Teeth of the Dog" (► 61). Also tennis, fishing, water sports, shooting, equestrian centers, polo training and yacht club.

✉ La Romana ☎ 523 3333; www.casadecampo.com.do

### ▼▼▼Coral Costa Caribe ($$)

Located in Juan Dolio, on the Caribbean coast and an easy 20-minute drive from Las Americas International Airport, this hotel complex is engulfed by vegetation and tropical flowers, bordering a palm-filled beach.

✉ San Pedro de Macoris, Juan Dolio ☎ 526 2244, www.coralhotels.com

### ▼▼▼Hotel Riu Palace Macao ($$–$$$)

A colonial-style resort, set within the Riu Resort with four other Riu hotels. A Caribbean Street features a spa, pizzeria, gym, jewelry, hairdresser, photography studio and lab, pharmacy, and more.

✉ Punta Cana Highway, Bavaro ☎ 221 7171

### ▼▼▼Oasis Canoa Hotel ($$–$$$)

All-inclusive resort with tropical architecture of stone, jute and punta-cana roofs, boasting big open spaces and overlooking the Caribbean Sea. A garden of island plants, includes the Bayahibe rose and the cotoperi. Small villas in the Taino-style are strides away from white sands and an intense blue sea.

✉ Playa Dominicus, Bayahibe ☎ 682 2662; www.globalia-hotels.com

### ✈✈✈ Oasis Hamaca ($–$$)

All-inclusive and the most popular in Boca Chica. Set right on its own beach, Boca Chica Bay is one of the country's most famous with a natural swimming lagoon protected by a reef. Great water sports and restaurants, plus a casino.

✉ Avenida Duarte, Boca Chica ☎ 523 4611; www.globalia-hotels.com

### ✈✈✈ Punta Cana Resort ($$–$$$)

See pages 78–79.

### The Sivory Punta Cana ($$$)

See pages 78–79.

## RESTAURANTS

### Capitan Cook Restaurant ($$)

One of the most famous restaurants of the Dominican Republic. Amazing seafood venue actually on the soft sands of the beach. Fresh lobster, shrimp, octopus and fish caught regularly and brought to the restaurant's cooler, in the shape of a treasure chest. Food is fried or grilled on stoves in the open.

✉ Playa El Cortecito, Nr. Higüey ☎ 552 0645 🕐 Noon–midnight

### ✈✈ El Concon Restaurante ($$)

See pages 58–59.

### ✈✈ Le Flamboyan ($$)

See pages 58–59.

### ✈✈ El Meson Español ($)

An al fresco restaurant set across from the beach, serving Spanish and Dominican food, soups and desserts. A good place to have an early snack or later, a romantic open-air dinner.

✉ Calle Boulevard, Juan Dolio ☎ 526 2666 🕐 Daily 11–11

### ✈✈ Neptuno's Club ($$$)

See pages 58–59.

### ▼▼Starei ($$)

Serving creole and shellfish specialties, this restaurant is set in the beautiful Altos de Chavón village (➤ 36). A gorgeous romantic setting and end to a day spent browsing round the village boutiques and art gallery.

✉ Altos de Chavón, La Romana ☎ 523 3333 🕓 Daily 11–11

## SHOPPING

### Altos de Chavón

There are artists' studios, a French bakery, souvenir boutiques, jewelry shops and a fashionable interior design, all set within this reconstructed Mediterranean village (➤ 36).

✉ Near Casa de Campo resort, La Romana ☎ 523 3333 🕓 Daily until late

### Boca Chica

Busy resort streets filled with typical Dominican souvenirs and Haitian paintings.

✉ Avenida Duarte, Boca Chica 🕓 Daily until late

### Domenico Premium Cigar Factory

Part cigar factory, part showroom, this emporium allows you to compare high-quality Dominican cigars and try before you buy.

✉ Avenida Domenico 6, Bavaro ☎ (1) 772 6873 for guided tour in English; www.domenicocigars.com 🕓 Mon–Fri 9–6

## ENTERTAINMENT

### Bávaro Disco

Famous club at Barceló Bávaro Beach Resort. If you're not a resident at the all-inclusive resort, you can always buy a day and night pass.

✉ Bávaro ☎ 686 5797 🕓 Weekends

### Club Génesis

A perfect way to end a day at this recreated medieval Mediterranean village. Ladies' and tequilla nights are popular.

✉ Altos de Chavón ☎ Via Casa de Campo 523 3333 🕓 Fri–Sat 11pm–4am

### Tropicalissimo Show
Leading Latin American and Caribbean music entertainment.
✉ Bávaro Casino, Barceló ☎ 221 6500

## SPORTS

### Mike's Marina Fishing Charter
This company has several boats and offers a full service guides
fishing experience with half or full-day charters possible.
✉ Bavaro Beach ☎ 552 1124; www.mikesmarina.info

### Pelicano Watersport
Pelicano offers dive training for the uninitiated and dive tours to
the great offshore locations for those already qualified. Plus they
have a whole range of other stuff – such as banana boat rides – at
their base on Bavaro Beach.
✉ Hotel Ocean Bavaro, Bavaro ☎ 221 0714; www.pelicanosport.com

### Punta Cana Lanes
Popular bowling alley with several lanes. There's pool and
electronic games area and an internet cafe on site.
✉ Plaza Bolera, Punta Cana ☎ 959 4444; www.pclanes.com
🕐 Mon–Fri 4pm–2am, Sat 1pm–2am, Sun 1pm–midnight

### Rancho Pat
Enjoy horseback riding on the beach at sunset or cross-country
trekking, Rancho Pat has a range of horses for all abilities.
✉ Hotel Sol de Plata, Bavaro Beach ☎ 223 8896

### Tropical Racing
Small karting track with almost a half a mile of tarmac. Karts can
be regulated depending on age and ability
✉ Route Cabeza del Torro, Bavaro ☎ 707 5164 🕐 Daily 10–10

# The Southwest and Cordillera Central

Bani

Barahona

**The west of the country is the Dominican Republic's unexplored frontier with vast tracts of land that have yet to see tourists in great number and are free of the huge all-inclusive hotels that line the eastern beaches.**

The southwest coast leading from Santo Domingo towards the Haitian border has many natural wonders to explore. The Baoruca Peninsula offers dry deserts interspersed with tropical peaks and the beaches are wild and unfettered with white-water spray breaking on the coastal rocks.

Inland, between the north and south coasts are the Cordillera Central, the country's rocky heartland and home to Pico Duarte, the Caribbean's highest peak. Conditions in the mountains were

ideal for the tobacco and coffee plantations that brought fame before the arrival of tourism. Today, the Cordillera are gaining a new lease of life with the seeds of eco-tourism already firmly planted.

Squeezed between the Baoruco Peninsula and the Cordillera is one of the country's most famous natural attractions. Lago Enriquillo and tiny Isla Cabritos with their populations of crocodiles and almost tame iguanas.

## AZUA DE COMPOSTELA

A convenient stopping point as you head further west, Azua de Compostela has a turbulent history. Founded in 1504 by Diego Velâsquez, who accompanied Christopher Columbus on his second voyage to Hispaniola, the town has seen many battles between Dominicans and Haitians (as well as earthquakes). The town park was created to honor those who fought for the area's independence in 1844.

✚ 14J 🚌 Express bus from Santo Domingo

## BANÍ

Baní lies off the main southwest route, the Carretera Sánchez. It's known for its small, sweet, red mangoes, though the area's varied agricultural produce also includes tomatoes, plantains, cashew nuts and red onions. Baní was the birthplace of General Máximo

Gómez, "the liberator of Cuba," who helped lead the revolution against the Spaniards and which resulted in Cuba's independence. Casa de Máximo Gómez is a museum devoted to the general. Strolling around Parque Duarte is very pleasant, and the salt pans of La Salinas, set among sand dunes, are around 45 minutes' drive away.

✚ 16K 🚌 *Gua-gua* from Santo Domingo

## BARAHONA

Barahona is a seaside town on the Península Pedernales, noted for its scientific reserves and its wildlife. Founded in 1802 by a Haitian and exploited for sugarcane by dictator Trujillo, Barahona still thrives on sugar – the chimneys spouting from the quivering plantations belong to the mills. Workers often set fire to parts of the fields so the stalks are easier to cut. The scene is pretty scary and the heat intense.

✚ 28R 🚌 Express bus from Santo Domingo ✈ María Montez, Barahon
ℹ Carreterra Batey Central ☎ 524 3650

### CONSTANZA

Ringed by glorious mountains, the town of Constanza stands at an altitude of about 4264ft (1,300m). It's a pretty, quiet place that makes an excellent base for walks. Many farms here belong to Japanese families brought in by Trujillo in the 1950s specifically to cultivate vegetables and fruit. Constanza is noted for its abundance of flowers, garlic and strawberries, growing in a picturesque valley.

✚ 6E ✉ La Vega

### CORDILLERA CENTRAL

Best places to see ➤ 40–41.

## ISLA CABRITOS

Isla Cabritos (Goat Island) takes its name from the goats that once grazed there. The island is 7.5 miles (12km) long and is within the small Parque Nacional Isla Cabritos. Combined with salty Lago Enriquillo and its American crocodiles (► 44), it makes for a fantastic day out. Used as a refuge and supply center for Indian chief Enriquillo, the island was ceded to a French family during the years of Haitian occupation. It was declared a national park in 1974. A round of dry, parched desert, the island is home to two species of iguana, the *ricordi* and the *rhinoceros*, which are unfortunately too friendly and run up to you expecting food. More than 106 types of plants have been recorded and 10 varieties of cactus which produce colorful flowers and 62 species of bird have been identified (45 native to the island). Remember to wear sturdy, covered footwear as scorpions scuttle in the sand.

✚ 26Q ✉ Parque Nacional Isla Cabritos ⏰ Daily 🎙 Moderate ❓ Permit required, must be accompanied by a guide

ℹ National parks office ☎ 472 3717

## an excursion

# drive and boat trip

This drive visits Lago Enriquillo (Lake Enriquillo) (➤ 44) and Parque Nacional Isla Cabritos (Isla Cabritos National Park), (➤ 143). Start early because morning is the best time to see the American crocodiles.

*Head west along Carretera 2, through the towns of San Cristóbal (➤ 150), Baní (➤ 140) and Azua de Compostela (➤ 140). The road changes to Carretera 44, and just before Barahona there's a right turn on to Carretera 48. At Neiba is the lake's loop road, paved and easy to follow; go either left or right.*

If you take the right side of the lake, look for Los Carritas, sad and happy faces in the rock above the road on the right hand side. Many people believe they date back to the Taino period. At the lake a small boat ferries you across to Isla Cabritos, followed by a half-hour walk to see the crocodiles, and probably a flock of pink flamingos launching into the sky. Later, cool off at the park's swimming pool and have an ice-cold drink from the bar.

*Continue to La Descubierta.*

Here you can have another swim in the sulphur pool, reached through a forest of tall, red mango trees.

*Retrace your route back to Santo Domingo.*

Tours previously visited the border with Haiti and an inexpensive market. However, US Department of State/UK

Foreign office guidelines advise against all but essential travel to Haiti. Aristide resigned in Feb 2004 amid mass protest and terrible violence. Dates for new elections were set several times during 2005 but finally held in Feb 2006 and won by one of Aristide's close allies, Rene Preval. It remains to be seen whether a new government can keep the county stable and improve economic conditions over the coming months and years. In the meantime, a UN security force is in place in the country.

**Distance** 179 miles (290km)
**Time** Full day
**Start/end point** Santo Domingo 🚌 18J ❓ Bring a sunhat, sunblock, mosquito repellent, drinking water and wear covered walking shoes **Lunch** Good choice on the road

## JARABACOA

Set in a sheltered mountain valley, Jarabacoa is best known for its waterfalls. Nowadays it's becoming more popular as a summer hilltop resort and hiking tourism center. Activities available include walks through the mountains and foothills, Jeep safaris, ballooning, bicycling and horseback riding, for example. You can swim in the refreshing pool, La Confluencia, in the Río Jimenoa (but be careful of the currents). Plus, of course, you can raft or just photograph Yaque del Norte, the longest and most important river, which descends as a series of waterfalls. Some 14 rivers have their source in the Cordillera Central. Many people visit Jarabacoa purely to see the waterfalls. By far the greatest is the 131ft (40m) El Salto de Jimenoa, which involves negotiating a steep trail and bridges to its edge. Another popular cascade is the shorter Salto de Baiguate that can be reached by foot or on horseback. Another deviation is the nearby Ramirez Factory, where a selection of the finest coffee beans for toasting is done by hand. There's a 45-minute tour, and you're welcome to taste the coffee.

🕂 6D ⊠ La Vega

ℹ Calle Estella Geraldino

☎ 14 573 7014

**Ramirez Factory**

🕐 Mon–Sat 8–6 (times vary)

☎ 574 2618

## LAGO ENRIQUILLO

Best places to see ➤ 44–45.

## PARQUE NACIONAL ARMANDO BERMÚDEZ & PARQUE NACIONAL JOSÉ DEL CARMEN RAMÍREZ

Since Columbus' arrival on the island of Hispaniola, it is estimated that two-thirds of the virgin forest in the Dominican Republic has been wiped out. Today Parque Nacional Armando Bermúdez (Armando Bermúdez National Park) and Parque Nacional José del Carmen Ramírez (José del Carmen Ramírez National Park) are the only remaining areas of extensive forests in these mountains. Their role of protection has helped towards retaining what's left and there's even a program of reforestation underway. In September 1998 Hurricane Georges destroyed river bridges and felled many pines. The bridges have since been rebuilt and the timber is being utilized. Naturally, the wildlife here abounds. Look for the Hispaniolan parrot, palm chats, doves and warblers. And, in more remote areas, wild boars forage.

🕂 4D–5E 👣 Inexpensive ❓ Permits required, tours and adventure travel

ℹ National parks office ☎ 472 3717

## PARQUE NACIONAL JARAGUA

Parque Nacional Jaragua (Jaragua National Park), at the southernmost tip of the country, is the largest protected area on the island. This is the place of the 4x4 vehicle, popular with birdwatchers, but remote. Principally dry forest, with two offshore islands, the park is hot and arid with beaches and a lagoon with a large flamingo colony. Among its birdlife 60 percent of the country's species are reportedly represented, along with iguanas, and the four marine turtles common here: hawksbill, leatherback, loggerhead and green. Undoubtedly there are yet more caves from the Taino period showing pictographs and petroglyphs.

✚ 26S ✉ Barahona Peninsula 🕓 Daily
✋ Inexpensive ❓ Organized tours are best
ℹ National parks office ☎ 472 3717

## PARQUE NACIONAL SIERRA DE BAORUCO

The aridity and isolation of Parque Nacional Sierra de Baoruco (also known as Parque Nacional Sierra de Bahoruco) may deter many visitors, but those who make the effort are treated to mountains as high as 7,764ft (2,367m), a plethora of birds and over 50 percent of all the country's native orchid species. Here, the

Taino Indian chief, Enriquillo, fought for his tribe's freedom against the Spaniards in the 1500s, declaring a small republic on top of the sierra.

🚩 26Q ⏲ Daily 8–5 🚌 Tour operator or *gua-gua* from Barahona

✋ Inexpensive

ℹ️ National parks office ☎ 472 3717

## PLAYA SAN RAFAEL

Dominicans from the capital often spend their leisure time at Playa San Rafael, chilling Presidente beer in the cool sulphur springs, before taking a dip in either the waterfall-fed lagoon or the sea. If you're hungry, don't worry because usually there's someone cooking fresh fish in the open air.

🚩 28R 🚌 *Gua-gua* from Barahona

## RESERVA ANTROPOLÓGICA DE LAS CUEVAS DE BORBÓN O DEL POMIER

The world's principal Taino archaeological location, Reserva Antropológica de las Cuevas de Borbón o del Pomier consists of 54 caves decorated with thousands of pictographs (wall drawings) and petroglyphs (rock carvings), as well as stalactites and stalagmites. Located 4 miles (7km) from San Cristóbal, near a limestone quarry, they were discovered in 1851 by Sir Robert Schonburgk, a British consul for the Dominican Republic. About a dozen caves are open for viewing. Cave Number One alone is blessed with 590 pictographs. Expect to also see aboriginal graves, ceramic and indigenous oddities (and a lot of bats).

➕ 17J ✉ Borbón Section, near San Cristóbal 🕐 Daily ✋ Inexpensive
ℹ National parks office ☎ 472 3717

## SAN CRISTÓBAL

San Cristóbal was the birthplace, in 1891, of dictator Rafael Leonidas Trujillo, who ruled the country ruthlessly from 1930 until his assassination in 1961. During his lifetime Trujillo transformed San Cristóbal into another of his showpieces. He lived in a country home called Casa de Caobas (the Mahogany House). Elsewhere, a dirt track winds uphill to Castillo de Cerro (the Mountain Castle) that he built but never inhabited after hearing someone remark on how hideous it looked. This ugly, dilapidated pale-yellow structure, stamped with white stars, remains in ruins and is so far not open to the public. It is, however, used by the neighborhood as a shelter during hurricanes.

Driving around the town takes you past jails so close to the road that you can see the inmates staring back at you. The neo-classical church, Parroquia de Nuestra Señora de Consolación, supposedly contained Trujillo's body in the family vault. Although he lay in state here, it's thought his corpse is buried in Pere Lachaise cemetery in Paris.

➕ 17K 🚌 Bus from Santo Domingo

## HOTELS

### Casa Bonita ($–$$)

This recently refurbished hotel comprises rustic cabins with air conditioning and hot water. Breakfast and dinner are included in the room rates. This is a laid-back place and nothing happens in much of a hurry – great if you want to slip into "island time".

✉ Calle Federico Geraldino 87 ☎ 476 5059; www.casabonita.dr

### Gran Jimenoa ($–$$)

This relatively new hotel set by the side of the River Jimenoa has spacious rooms with air conditioning, televisions and balconies set around a courtyard. The facilities include a pool and a hot tub. Adventure tours can be arranged from the front desk.

✉ Avenida La Confluencia, Los Corralitos, Jarabacoa ☎ 574 6304; www.granjimenoa.com

### Hodelpa Centro Plaza Hotel ($$–$$$)

One of the largest hotels in Santiago de los Cabelleros, it provides a number of luxurious touches including a small gym and a massage center. The Alta Vista Restaurant on the top floor offers panoramic views across the city. The Tanari Disco Club is open nightly with live shows Tuesday and Thursday.

✉ Calle Mella 54, Santiago de los Cabelleros ☎ 581 7000; www.hodelpa.com

### Hotel Costa Larimar ($$–$$$)

Set on a good sandy beach, this is the only all-inclusive resort in this part of the country. While facilities are not as varied as some of the east coast resorts the rates are less expensive and it makes a comfortable choice for exploring this area of the country.

✉ Highway 44, Bahoruco ☎ 524 1111; www.hotelcostalarimar.com

### Hotel Playa Pelenque ($)

Sitting close to the beach and surrounded by unspoiled natural countryside, from here you can take trips to the Haitian border or into the Cordillera Central. Rooms are simple but clean with air conditioning. There is a pool, restaurant and a tropical garden.

✉ Playa Pelenque ☎ 341 8462

### Rancho Baiguate ($)

Safari-style ranch with a swimming pool backed by mountains. Lunch is a typical Dominican-style buffet with organically grown vegetables and fruit. Excursions are available and include treks into the mountains, rafting and horseback riding.

✉ Jarabacoa ☎ 574 6890

## RESTAURANTS

### Asadero los Robles ($)

Very popular with the local crowd, this rustic eatery serves very tasty grilled meats and seafood at value for money prices. In the evening the *merengue* and *bachata* gets very loud – great Dominican atmosphere.

✉ Avenida Enriquillo, Baharona ☎ 524 1629 ⏲ Daily 10–late

### Brisas del Caribe ($–$$)

This open-sided restaurant is the smartest address in town and true to its name is cooled by the Caribbean breezes. The extensive menu will satisfy the most finicky of tastes, but as always here, the seafood wins most prizes.

✉ Avenida Enriquillo, Barahona ☎ 524 2794 ⏲ Daily 9am–11pm

### Chichita ($)

The most popular choice for snacks or a full meal in the town, Chichita is a full on Dominican eatery serving delicious and inexpensive plates of rice and beans with a range of grilled meats and chicken. Locals stop by for a *pastales en hoja,* a Dominican empenada that comes in various flavours.

✉ Avenida Padre Ayala, San Cristobal ☎ 528 3012 ⏲ Daily 9am–midnight

### Kukara Macara ($$)

This country and western style bar and restaurant has a good range of snacks and main courses. There's a great line in Tex-Mex food with burritos and tacos plus sandwiches; or you can order substantial steaks and meat dishes if you have a big appetite.

✉ Avenida Francia, Zona Monumental, Santiago de los Cabelleros

☎ 241 3143; www.kukaramacara.com ⏲ Daily 8am–11pm

### Restaurante Luz ($–$$)

In the center of town but overlooking the coast, the upstairs dining room has pretty views and catches the cooling breeze. The menu concentrates on fresh seafood served with rice and beans.

✉ Calle del Playa, Bahoruco ☎ 630 9861 ◷ Daily 8am–11pm

### Restaurant El Rancho ($$)

Fish, seafood, steaks, chicken. Specialties are chicken stuffed with sweet plantains, crêpes with seafood, watercress soup. Also pizzas and sandwiches.

✉ Jarabacoa ☎ 574 4557 ◷ Daily until late

### Tipico Bonao ($–$$)

On the road between Santo Domingo and Santiago, it's been a well known landmark on the route since the 1960s. The décor is appealing, the service polite and the food, which includes all the Dominican favorites and some international dishes, is delicious, bringing in a constant stream of road-weary travelers.

✉ Autopista Duarte, Km 83, Bonao ◷ 248 7924 ◷ Daily 7am–midnight

## SHOPPING

### Melo Coffee Factory

The coffee produced in the Cordillera Central is some of the best coffee in the world, buying direct from the factory means it can't get any fresher.

✉ Calle Anacaona, Barahona ☎ 524 2440 ◷ Mon–Sat 8–5

### Mercado Modelo

The liveliest market in the region, this emporium sells souvenirs and foods for a picnic in the country.

✉ Calle des Sol, Santiago de los Caballeros ◷ Mon–Fri 9–5

# Index

# Acknowledgements

The Automobile Association wishes to thank the following photographers, companies and picture libraries for their assistance in the preparation of this book.

Abbreviations for the picture credits are as follows – (t) top; (b) bottom; (l) left; (r) right; (c) centre; (AA) AA World Travel Library

**4l** Playa Dominicus, AA/C Sawyer; **4c** Scarves for sale, Cabarete, AA/C Sawyer; **4r** Altos de Chavon, AA/C Sawyer; **5l** Casa de Campo, AA/L Karen Stow; **5c** Parque Colon, AA/C Sawyer; **6/7** Playa Dominicus, AA/C Sawyer; **8/9** Carnival, Santo Domingo, AA/C Sawyer; **10/11** Beach scene, AA/L Karen Stow; **10c** Bavaro, AA/C Sawyer; **10bl** Parque Colon, Santo Domingo, AA/C Sawyer; **10br** Monte Criste, AA/C Sawyer; **11c** La Cienega Valley, AA/C Sawyer; **11b** Mural, AA/C Sawyer; **12/13t** San Pedro de Marcoris, AA/C Sawyer; **12/13b** Market in Bani, AA/C Sawyer; **13cl** Fruit Stall, AA/C Sawyer; **13cr** Barahona, fish, AA/C Sawyer; **13b** Plantains cooking, AA/C Sawyer; **14/15** Rum, AA/C Sawyer; **14** Drinking coconut milk, AA/C Sawyer; **15l** Presidente Beer, AA/C Sawyer; **15r** Playa Bonita, AA/C Sawyer; **16/17t** Zona Colonial, AA/L Karen Stow; **16/17b** Lake Enriquillo, AA/L Karen Stow; **16t** Rincon Beach, Las Galeras, AA/C Sawyer; **16b** Merengue Dancing, AA/C Sawyer; **18/19** Gray Whale, AA/P Bennett; **18** Bavaro beach, AA/C Sawyer; **19** Tobacco drying, AA/C Sawyer; **20/21** Scarves for sale, Cabarete, AA/C Sawyer; **24/25** Cabarete, AA/C Sawyer; **26/27** Cruise Liner, AA/D Lyons; **28** Bus, Punta Cana, AA/C Sawyer; **30** Newspaper Stand, AA/C Sawyer; **31** Phone Box, AA/C Sawyer; **32** Las Terrenas, AA/C Sawyer; **34/35** Altos de Chavon, AA/C Sawyer; **36t** Altos de Chavon, AA/C Sawyer; **36/37** Amphitheatre, Altos de Chavon, AA/C Sawyer; **37** Altos de Chavon, AA/C Sawyer; **38t** Whale Watching, AA/C Sawyer; **38c** Whale watching, AA/L Karen Stow; **38/39** Levandato Island, AA/C Sawyer; **39** Playa Bonita, AA/C Sawyer; **40** La Cienega Valley, AA/C Sawyer; **40/41** El Salto de Jimenoa, AA/C Sawyer; **41** Constanza, AA/C Sawyer; **42/43t** Soana Island, AA/L Karen Stow; **42/43b** Isla Saona, AA/L Karen Stow; **44t** Statue of Enriquillo a Tainos, AA/C Sawyer; **44b** Crocodile, Lago Enriquillo, AA/L Karen Stow; **45** Iguana, Lago Enriquillo, AA/C Sawyer; **46/47** Monument to the Heroes, AA/L Karen Stow; **48/49** Parque Nacional la Isabella, AA/L Karen Stow; **49t** Cemetery, Parque Nacional la Isabella, AA/L Karen Stow; **49b** Columbus Museum, Parque Nacional la Isabella, AA/L Karen Stow; **50** Bavara Beach, AA/C Sawyer; **50/51t** Bavaro Beach, AA/C Sawyer; **50/51b** Bavaro Beach, AA/C Sawyer; **52** Bahia de Puerto Plata, AA/C Sawyer; **52/53t** Puerto Plata, AA/C Sawyer; **52/53b** Parque Luperon, AA/C Sawyer; **54/55t** Zona Colonial, AA/L Karen Stow; **54/55b** Fortaleza Ozamal, AA/L Karen Stow; **55** Zona Colonial, AA/L Karen Stow; **56/57** Casa de Campo, AA/L Karen Stow; **58/59** Breakfast, AA/L Karen Stow; **61** Robert Trent Golf Course, Playa Dorada, AA/L Karen Stow; **62/63** Bavaro Beach, AA/C Sawyer; **64/65** Sea Turtle, AA/P Aithie; **66/67** Scuba Diving, AA/C Sawyer; **69** Pico Isabel de Torres, AA/L Karen Stow; **70** Museo de Amber, AA/C Sawyer; **70/71** Cathedral San Felipe Apostel, AA/C Sawyer; **71** Constanza, AA/C Sawyer; **73** Cordillera Central, AA/L Karen Stow; **74** Santo Domingo, Carnival, AA/C Sawyer; **76** Santo Domingo, AA/L Karen Stow; **77** Cabarete, AA/L Karen Stow; **78** Hotel Room, Stockbyte; **80/81** Parque Colon, AA/C Sawyer; **83** Museo Alcazar de Colon, AA/C Sawyer; **84** Puerta El Conde, Santo Domingo, AA/L Karen Stow; **84/85** Catedral de Santa Maria la Menor, AA/C Sawyer; **86** Faro de Colon, AA/L Karen Stow; **88t** Fortalexa Ozama, Santo Domingo, AA/C Sawyer; **88c** Fortzaleza Ozama, Santo Domingo, AA/C Sawyer; **89** Museum Alcazar de Colon, Santiago, AA/C Sawyer; **90** Fortaleza Ozama, Santo Domingo, AA/C Sawyer; **90/91** Plaza de la Hispanidad, AA/C Sawyer; **92** Museo Alcazar de Las Atarazanas, AA/C Sawyer; **92/93** Museo de las Casa Reales, AA/L Karen Stow; **93** Museo de las Casas Reales, AA/L Karen Stow; **94** Museo de la Hombre Dominicano, AA/C Sawyer; **94/95** Amber Museum, Santo Domingo, AA/L Karen Stow; **96/97** Parque Colon, AA/L Karen Stow; **97** Parque Colon, AA/C Sawyer; **98** Ruinas de Hospital San Nicolas de Bari, AA/L Karen Stow; **105** Surfboards, Cabarete, AA/C Sawyer; **106t** Cabarete Beach, AA/C Sawyer; **106b** San Felipe Fort, AA/C Sawyer; **107** Caya Lavantado, AA/C Sawyer; **108/109** Laguna Gri Gri, AA/C Sawyer; **109** Museo de Amber, AA/C Sawyer; **110** Parque Luperon AA/L Karen Stow; **111** Parque Luperon, AA/L Karen Stow; **112/113** Puerto Chiquito, AA/C Sawyer; **113** Amber Museum, Puerto Plata, AA/L Karen Stow; **114t** El Morro Peak, AA/C Sawyer; **114b** Torre del Paine, AA/L Karen Stow; **115** Playa Dorada, AA/L Karen Stow; **116** Sugar Cane field, Santiago de Los Cabarellos, AA/C Sawyer; **116/117** Sugar Cane fields, AA/C Sawyer; **117** Sociedad Centro de Recreo, AA/C Sawyer; **118/119** Playa Chiquito, AA/C Sawyer; **119t** Las Terrenas, AA/C Sawyer; **119b** Las Terrenas, AA/C Sawyer; **125** Boca Chica, AA/C Sawyer; **126** Basilica de Nuestra Senora de la Altagracia, AA/C Sawyer; **126/127** Bayahibe, AA/L Karen Stow; **128/129** Casa de Campo, AA/L Karen Stow; **128** Casa de Campo, AA/L Karen Stow; **130/131** Isla Soano, AA/L Karen Stow; **132t** Parque Nacional Submarino La Caleta, AA/L Karen Stow; **132c** Parque Nacional Submarino La Caleta, AA/L Karen Stow; **133t** Boca Chica, AA/C Sawyer; **133b** Boca Chica, AA/C Sawyer; **134t** Sammy Sosa Statue, AA/L Karen Stow; **134b** San Pedro de Macorios, AA/L Karen Stow; **139** Playa San Rafael, AA/L Karen Stow; **140** Bani, market, AA/C Sawyer; **141t** Museo de Maximo Gomez, AA/C Sawyer; **141b** Bahia de Neiba, AA/C Sawyer; **142** Constanza, AA/C Sawyer; **142/143** Isla Cabritos, AA/L Karen Stow; **144/145** Isla Cabritos, AA/L Karen Stow; **146/147** Jarabacoa, AA/L Karen Stow; **147** Coffee beans, Jarabacoa, AA/L Karen Stow; **148/149t** Laguna de Oviedo, AA/C Sawyer; **148/149b** Playa San Rafael, AA/C Sawyer; **151** Iglesia de San Cristobal, AA/C Sawyer

Every effort has been made to trace the copyright holders, and we apologise in advance for any accidental errors. We would be happy to apply the corrections in the following edition of this publication.

# Sight locator list

This index relates to the maps on the covers. We have given map references to the main sights in the book. Grid references in italics indicate sights featured on the town plan. Some sights within towns may not be plotted on the maps.

# Dear Reader

**Your comments, opinions and recommendations are very important to us. Please help us to improve our travel guides by taking a few minutes to complete this simple questionnaire.**

*You do not need a stamp (unless posted outside the UK). If you do not want to cut this page from your guide, then photocopy it or write your answers on a plain sheet of paper.*

Send to: **The Editor, AA World Travel Guides,**
**FREEPOST SCE 4598, Basingstoke RG21 4GY.**

### Your recommendations...

We always encourage readers' recommendations for restaurants, nightlife or shopping – if your recommendation is used in the next edition of the guide, we will send you a **FREE AA Guide** of your choice from this series. Please state below the establishment name, location and your reasons for recommending it.

_____

_____

_____

_____

_____

Please send me **AA Guide** _____

### About this guide...

Which title did you buy?

AA _____

Where did you buy it? _____

When? m m / y y

Why did you choose this guide? _____

_____

_____

_____

_____

Did this guide meet your expectations?

Exceeded ☐   Met all ☐   Met most ☐   Fell below ☐

Were there any aspects of this guide that you particularly liked? _____

_____

_____

_____

*continued on next page...*

Is there anything we could have done better? _____
_____
_____
_____

## About you...
Name (Mr/Mrs/Ms) _____
Address _____
_____
_____ Postcode _____

Daytime tel nos _____
Email _____

Please only give us your mobile phone number or email if you wish to hear from us about
other products and services from the AA and partners by text or mms, or email.

Which age group are you in?
Under 25 ☐   25–34 ☐   35–44 ☐   45–54 ☐   55–64 ☐   65+ ☐

How many trips do you make a year?
Less than one ☐   One ☐   Two ☐   Three or more ☐

Are you an AA member? Yes ☐   No ☐

## About your trip...
When did you book? m m / y y       When did you travel? m m / y y

How long did you stay? _____

Was it for business or leisure? _____

Did you buy any other travel guides for your trip? _____

If yes, which ones? _____
_____
_____

Thank you for taking the time to complete this questionnaire. Please send it to us as soon as
possible, and remember, you do not need a stamp (unless posted outside the UK).

**AA** Travel Insurance call 0800 072 4168 or visit www.theAA.com